In Seven Days

In Seven Days

Jordi Mand

In Seven Days
first published 2025 by Scirocco Drama
An imprint of J. Gordon Shillingford Publishing Inc.

Scirocco Drama Editor: Glenda MacFarlane
Cover design by Doowah Design
Author photo by Dahlia Katz
Production photos by Dahlia Katz.

Printed and bound in Canada on 100% post-consumer recycled paper.

Production inquiries to:
Ian Arnold
Catalyst TCM Inc.
ian@catalysttcm.com
416-568-8673

Library and Archives Canada Cataloguing in Publication

Title: In seven days / Jordi Mand.
Names: Mand, Jordi, author.
Identifiers: Canadiana 20250181797 | ISBN 9781990738678 (softcover)
Subjects: LCGFT: Drama.
Classification: LCC PS8626.A519 I6 2025 | DDC C812/.6—dc23

J.Gordon Shillingford Publishing respectfully acknowledges that we are located in Winnipeg, which is on Treaty 1 territory, the traditional lands of the Anishinaabe, Cree, Oji-Cree, Dene, and Dakota Peoples, and the homeland of the Métis Nation.

We acknowledge the financial support of the Canada Council for the Arts, the Government of Canada, the Manitoba Arts Council, and the Manitoba Government for our publishing program.

J. Gordon Shillingford Publishing
P.O. Box 86, RPO Corydon Avenue, Winnipeg, MB Canada R3M 3S3

To my parents – thank you for everything.

And I mean it from the bottom of my heart.

Jordi Mand

Jordi Mand is known for her impactful contributions to the worlds of theatre and television. Her plays, including *Between the Sheets, Caught, This Will Be Excellent, Brontë: The World Without*, and a new stage adaptation of the literary classic *Little Women,* have been translated and published internationally. Mand has collaborated with many of Canada's most prominent theatre companies, such as the Stratford Festival, the Royal Manitoba Theatre Centre, The Grand Theatre, Theatre Passe Muraille, Nightwood Theatre, the Harold Green Jewish Theatre Company, and many more. She was a writer for the hit CTV drama *Cardinal* and has participated in numerous development rooms for Canadian television shows. She is a graduate of the National Theatre School of Canada and the Canadian Film Centre's Bell Prime Time TV Program. Mand resides in Toronto with her husband, daughter, and a cat who eats way too much.

Acknowledgements

I am deeply indebted to the following people:

To the team at the Harold Green Jewish Theatre Company—Avery Saltzman, David Eisner, and Matt Birnbaum—who first commissioned *In Seven Days* and remained an unwavering source of support, encouragement, and enthusiasm throughout its entire journey.

To the team at The Grand Theatre—Dennis Garnhum, who championed the play as part of his final season, and Rachel Peake, whose leadership, along with her incredible team, ensured the production was handled with such care. Special thanks to Evan Klassen, Lyndee Hansen, Christine Gruenbauer, Breanne Ritchie, Lia Karidas, and Melissa Mae Shipley for their dedication behind the scenes.

To my director and dramaturge, Philip Akin, whose collaboration was a dream from start to finish.

To the actors who lent their voices and talents to the play's early development—Hannah Miller, Alon Nashman, Amy Rutherford, Ralph Small, Mazin Elsadig, and Emilio Vieira.

To the incredible cast and creative team who brought the premiere production to life with such heart—Shaina Silver-Baird, Ron Lea, Mairi Babb, Ralph Small, and Brendan McMurtry-Howlett, along with Sean Mulcahy, Siobhan Sleath, Lyon Smith, Amanda Nicholls, Suzanne McArthur, and Kelse Rae.

To my agent, Ian Arnold, for being there every step of the way.

To Glenda MacFarlane and the team at Scirocco Drama for bringing *In Seven Days* to life in print, ensuring its journey continues beyond the stage.

To my Brookfield team for their support throughout this journey. Special thanks to Sachin Shah, Tom Corbett, Lyndsay Hatlelid, Agostino De Gasperis, and Soraya Pimenta for their thoughtfulness along the way.

To my religious consultant on the play, Rabbi Debra Dressler, whose insights, knowledge, and generosity added immeasurable depth to the play.

To my family, Jason Mandlowitz, Daryl Fridenberg, and Zach Mandlowitz, without whom this play – and all my plays, really – would not exist.

And to my sweethearts, Marcus and Gilah, for being my entire world.

Playwright's Notes

Several years ago, a family friend qualified for MAID (Medical Assistance in Dying) and made the decision to go through with it. He was my father's childhood friend and a deeply involved member of the London Jewish community, so his choice reverberated far beyond his immediate family. It was a decision that sparked difficult, deeply personal conversations among those who knew him.

I remember discussing it with my brother, who said, "I don't understand how someone could choose to do something like that." In response, I asked him a question that had been weighing on me: if our father—who we both love and adore—were ever in the same situation, would he feel the same way? Without hesitation, he said, "Yes." And part of me understood exactly where he was coming from. The thought of losing a parent, even on their own terms, is almost unbearable.

But as someone who has faced serious health challenges myself, and who has watched my husband, mother, and grandparents navigate their own, I also understood the other side. I understood the relief that MAID can offer, the autonomy it provides, and the unimaginable strength it takes to make such a decision.

That tension—between holding on and letting go, between love and personal autonomy—is where *In Seven Days* was born.

This play is, at its heart, about family. It's about how, as children, we learn to say goodbye, and how, as parents, we wrestle with the responsibility of doing what is best for ourselves, even when it hurts the ones we love most.

Foreword

Throughout history, Judaism has prohibited almost any action that accelerates death—even removing a pillow from underneath a dying patient's head. This was to ensure that even the dying maintain their humanity. Life itself is understood to be a gift from God, and to hasten death is to violate the commandment LO TIRTZACH—do not murder.

But even in these ancient contexts, there was an understanding that we mustn't create obstacles to death; we bear the responsibility to prevent needless suffering. Impediments to dying, whether efficacious prayer or medical treatment, must also be removed.

Today's medical landscape leaves us at odds with these competing values. Technologies created to sustain life become unintended obstacles to a dignified death. Medical Assistance in Dying seeks to bridge these obstacles, giving a person with incurable illness the agency to bypass them in a just, humane manner.

Liberal religious denominations, like the Judaism at the foundation of Sam's (family's) story, are rising to meet the challenge resulting from life-extending technologies. Some find a way to accept medically assisted dying within the centuries of religious law. Others do not, yet admonish us not to judge the person who does choose this path, nor deny them any honour in death.

In my pastoral work (as a rabbi), I often find that people facing death, and the ones who love them, are on different journeys. *In Seven Days* captures those journeys, their unique twists and turns, painful touchpoints, and their ultimate convergence as Sam's family not only makes peace with his decision but is able lovingly to embrace and accompany him in his final moments.

We may consider ourselves rational beings, but we live our lives emotionally. Rabbi Eli personifies the voice of tradition—do not murder—but he does so through the lens of a lifelong friendship that transcends his rabbinic role. Sam's life partner, Shelley, embodies the anguish of a spouse watching her love's decline in body and spirit. And Sam's daughter Rachel, approaching her own life milestones, helps us "catch up" to that pre-existent reality in the few days she is given to prepare.

Jordi blends her creative insight with the lived experience of a mother, daughter, partner and friend to animate these crisscrossing emotional journeys. Through the voices of Sam and his family, we hear our own heartache. Our laughter over poppy seed bagels and bridesmaid dresses is a welcome balm as we bond our hearts to the characters' experiences. Love gets the final word during the tearful goodbyes, and our hearts are full.

In this "comedy about death," we still affirm the beauty of life.

If you've ever faced an illness, the loss of a loved one, and especially the loss of a parent, you will recognize these emotional landscapes and their accompanying states.

Each character from *In Seven Days* comes to their bittersweet understanding at a different time, and in a different way.

But this is the story of love. Love of family, romantic love, love of faith. Love of life.

Do we honour our lives by extending them as long as possible? Or by living them with dignity without regrets? Saying goodbye is difficult, but inevitable.

In Seven Days is a story about life, pain, hope, expectations.

A story about love.

All communities of faith are grappling with these questions. The answers vary…

How they frame the question.

Motive matters—but the motive to end suffering does not supersede a motive to cause a person's life to end.

Placing love before judgement. Honouring the sacrifices Sam has made, by being willing to sacrifice the added time with him that would undoubtedly bring him suffering.

And lost dignity.

What may have once happened in hushed conversations is now in the open, as is our struggle to navigate.

Rabbi Debra Stahlberg Dressler
Spring 2025

Rabbi Dressler was the Religious Consultant for In Seven Days

Production History

The first production of *In Seven Days* was a co-production by The Grand Theatre and the Harold Green Jewish Theatre company. The play premiered at the Grand Theatre in London, Ontario, February 13–March 2, 2024, with the following cast and creative team:

Cast

Shelley: .... Mairi Babb

Sam: .... Ron Lea

Darren: .... Brendan McMurtry-Howlett

Rachel: .... Shaina Silver-Baird

Eli: .... Ralph Small

Creative Team

Director: .... Philip Akin

Set and Costume Design: .... Sean Mulcahy

Lighting Design: .... Siobhán Sleath

Sound Design: .... Lyon Smith

Assistant Director: .... Amanda Nicholls

Religious Consultant: .... Rabbi Debra Dressler

Stage Manager: .... Suzanne McArthur

Assistant Stage Manager: .... Kelsey Rae

Apprentice Stage Manager: .... Sydney Stobo

Stage Management Student: .... Lara Campbell

This production of *In Seven Days* then moved to the Meridian Arts Centre in Toronto as part of the Harold Green Jewish Theatre Company's 2023/24 season, where it ran from May 4 to May 16, 2024.

Characters

RACHEL:	Mid-thirties, daughter of SAM
SAM:	Sixties, father of RACHEL
SHELLEY:	Early forties, partner of SAM
ELI:	Sixties, rabbi and friend of SAM
DARREN:	Mid-thirties, ex-boyfriend of RACHEL

Time

Now.

Setting

A smaller city in Ontario, like London.

Notes on Text and Production

The play runs 80 minutes, with no intermission.

Ellipsis (…) indicates when a character stops herself/himself or has a change in thought.

Dash (—) indicates when a character is being cut off by another character.

Slash (/) indicates when characters are speaking over each other.

Rachel (Shaina Silver-Baird) grapples with the devastating news that her father, Sam (Ron Lea), has qualified for MAID and is determined to proceed. Photograph by Dahlia Katz.

Lifelong friends Sam (Ron Lea) and Eli (Ralph Small) share a heartfelt laugh, reminiscing about the past as Eli gently questions Sam's life-altering choice. Photograph by Dahlia Katz.

Amidst the chaos of wedding preparations, Shelley (Mairi Babb) insists Rachel (Shaina Silver-Baird) try on dresses—just as Rachel's ex, Darren (Brendan McMurtry-Howlett), arrives unexpectedly. Photograph by Dahlia Katz.

Eli (Ralph Small) officiates the beautiful and intimate wedding of Sam (Ron Lea) and Shelley (Mairi Babb). Photograph by Dahlia Katz.

Darren (Brendan McMurtry-Howlett) offers Rachel (Shaina Silver-Baird) comfort as she struggles to make sense of the overwhelming emotions surrounding her. Photograph by Dahlia Katz.

In a final, desperate plea, Rachel (Shaina Silver-Baird) begs her father, Sam (Ron Lea), to reconsider his decision. Photograph by Dahlia Katz.

Surrounded by his loved ones, Sam (Ron Lea) shares a final goodbye with Rachel (Shaina Silver-Baird), Shelley (Mairi Babb), Eli (Ralph Small), and Darren (Brendan McMurtry-Howlett). Photograph by Dahlia Katz.

After Sam's passing, Rachel (Shaina Silver-Baird) and Shelley (Mairi Babb) sit together in quiet reflection, searching for a way forward. Photograph by Dahlia Katz.

Day 1

Late afternoon.

The main floor of a suburban bungalow. The layout is open, with a kitchen, eating area, and living room off the front door of the house. There are several other rooms (bedrooms, bathrooms) that are not visible. The walls and cabinets are covered in tasteful Judaica paintings, prints, and trinkets. There is a scattering of picture frames of family members around the house.

The living room and kitchen are empty. From offstage the garage door closes as if someone enters the house.

RACHEL: *(Offstage.)* Hello?

From offstage we hear someone kicking off their shoes.

(Offstage.) Hello?

After a moment, RACHEL enters the space. She's dressed professionally in a tailored pantsuit. She looks overworked, overtired, and frazzled. She's carrying a very large and very full paper bag.

Dad?

She puts the bag on the counter. It's so full that the bag immediately starts to tumble over.

RACHEL catches it just before the contents spill out. She repositions the bag on the counter, pulls out her phone, and checks her email.

RACHEL: Hello? Dad?

SHELLEY: *(Offstage.)* Shhh!

SHELLEY appears from one of the bedrooms. She's meticulous about her appearance. Her makeup is fully done, her hair is newly dyed, and she has a fresh manicure.

Keep your voice down. He's sleeping.

RACHEL: Something's wrong with the garage door.

SHELLEY: What?

RACHEL: It won't open properly.

SHELLEY: What do you mean it won't open properly?

RACHEL: I put in the code and/

SHELLEY: What about the remote/

RACHEL: I don't have a remote. You took mine when you lost yours/

SHELLEY: I thought your father gave you another one/

RACHEL: He didn't. I've been using the panel on the door/

SHELLEY: And the panel didn't work/

RACHEL: No. That's what I'm trying to tell you. I punched the code in over and over again and it took forever to—

SHELLEY: Well, I don't know anything about the garage. You'll have to speak to your father about that. *(Looking RACHEL over.)* Are you alone?

RACHEL: Yes.

SHELLEY: You didn't bring the boyfriend?

RACHEL: No. He has a gig.

SHELLEY: A gig?

RACHEL: He's playing at a club tomorrow night.

SHELLEY: And he couldn't reschedule?

RACHEL: No, Shelley. He's headlining a DJ night. And it's sold out. They can't just reschedule. And… we broke up.

SHELLEY: Broke up? Did he break up with you or did you break up with—

RACHEL: I don't want to talk about it—

SHELLEY: I'm just wondering whose decision it was—

RACHEL: I really don't want to—

SHELLEY: Because it makes a difference who broke up with—

RACHEL: Shelley, I said don't want to talk about it, okay?

SHELLEY: Okay. Okay. Fine.

She unpacks the paper bag and pulls out a number of smaller plastic bags all filled with bagels.

They're poppy seed. They're all poppy seed. Where's the sesame?

RACHEL: That's all they had left.

SHELLEY: All they had left… What time did you go?

RACHEL: On my way out of town.

SHELLEY: What time was that?

RACHEL: Around two.

SHELLEY: Well, that's the problem, isn't it? You went after lunch. You can't go after lunch. All they'll have left after lunch are the ones that people don't want… which are poppy seed.

RACHEL: I went when I could.

SHELLEY: You couldn't go before lunch?

RACHEL: I had a meeting at work and didn't think that picking up bagels was a good enough reason to cancel it.

SHELLEY: What am I going to do with all of these?

RACHEL: I don't know. Eat them?

SHELLEY: I can't eat these. They're poppy seed.

RACHEL: Does it really matter?

SHELLEY: If you knew anything about bagels—

RACHEL: It's a seed, Shelley. It doesn't change anything.

SHELLEY: Rachel, it changes everything.

RACHEL: You said pick up six dozen bagels. You did not say pick up six dozen sesame seed—

SHELLEY: Yes, I did. I would never tell you to buy six dozen poppy seed bagels. Never. How am I going to take these to Temple tomorrow? What will people think?

RACHEL: I'm sure they'll just be happy to have something to eat.

SHELLEY: Clearly, you've never been to kiddush after Shabbat service.

These people are animals. If they don't have their sesame seed bagels—

RACHEL: Can't you just pick up some bagels here, then?

SHELLEY: They don't sell bagels like these here. The bagels here taste like cardboard. No one likes the bagels here. If we bring Montreal-style bagels to Temple it gives us clout.

RACHEL: Bagels give you clout?

SHELLEY: Yes. But only if they're sesame.

RACHEL: They're just bagels. Who fucking cares?

SHELLEY: Rachel! Language!

RACHEL: It's not going to matter to anyone.

SHELLEY: I had to serve poppy seed rugelach a few weeks back because I couldn't find any other flavours. And Mrs. Hurtzman almost spit in my face when she saw that poppy seed was the only option.

RACHEL: I'm sure Mrs. Hurtzman got over it.

SHELLEY: Oh, she got over it all right. Just enough to remind me about it every time I see her.

RACHEL: Then don't bring them.

SHELLEY: I have to bring them. I'm on bagel duty this week. This is a disaster.

RACHEL: I'm pretty sure there are worse things in life than having to eat a fucking poppy seed bagel.

SHELLEY: Language!

RACHEL: You didn't tell me you were serving them. I thought they were for you.

SHELLEY: You thought I would be eating six dozen poppy seed bagels on my own. Am I some kind of monster?

SAM shuffles on stage from one of the bedrooms. He wears an old sweatsuit. He walks with one cane and moves with great effort.

SAM: What's going on in here?

SHELLEY holds up the bags of bagels for SAM to see.

SHELLEY: Poppy seed. She brought poppy seed bagels.

SAM: You have something against sesame seeds now?

RACHEL: I have nothing against anything.

SAM: What happened to sesame?

RACHEL: Oh my god.

SHELLEY: What am I going to do with six dozen poppy seed bagels?

RACHEL: *(To SAM.)* Hi.

She goes to SAM and kisses him on the cheek. SHELLEY grabs a knife and aggressively starts to unpack the bagels.

SHELLEY: And now I have to serve poppy seed bagels to a mob of angry, petty, ungrateful—

SAM: They're not ungrateful.

SHELLEY: Oh, yes, they are. All they care about is being fed. They don't care what kind of effort you had to make to prepare everything for them. And would it kill someone to say thank you from time to time?

SAM: Do you want some help with those?

SHELLEY: Sam, I know how to cut a bagel.

SAM: I know you do. In fact, no one cuts a bagel better than you do.

SHELLEY: And I'm the only one who volunteers to bring anything every week, and be there to set up, and clean everything up at the end.

SAM: *(To RACHEL.)* How was the drive?

RACHEL: I hit some traffic, but it was fine.

SHELLEY: Well, if you left earlier… in time to get sesame seed bagels then—

RACHEL: I left as early as I could. *(To SAM.)* She's in a mood.

SHELLEY: I can hear you.

RACHEL: *(To SAM)* The garage door isn't working.

SAM: The code isn't working?

RACHEL: No. I had to type it in five or six times before it would—

SHELLEY: Why don't you just use the front door?

RACHEL: Because you asked me to use the garage so I wouldn't track dirt or mud throughout your entire—

SHELLEY: Is trying to keep the house clean a crime?

SAM: What code did you use?

RACHEL: 1804. The only code you have.

SAM: Is that the code?

RACHEL: It's the only one I've ever used. Mom's birthday, right?

SHELLEY: Your mother's.... *(To SAM.)* You never told me that.

SAM: Never told you what?

SHELLEY: That Barbara's birthday was the code for the garage.

SAM: I didn't think of it.

SHELLEY: It would have been nice to know that your ex-wife's birthday was the code to the—

RACHEL: She's not his ex-wife. Why do you always say that/

SHELLEY: Technically/

RACHEL: No. Not technically. They didn't get divorced. Mom died. There's a huge difference/

SHELLEY: Regardless, I would have liked to know something like that.

SAM: It didn't even cross my mind.

SHELLEY: Apparently.

SAM: *(To RACHEL.)* Is it just you? You didn't bring the boyfriend?

SHELLEY: They broke up.

RACHEL: Shelley!

SHELLEY: Well, did you or did you not break up?

RACHEL: Yes. But you don't have to—

SAM: When?

SHELLEY: She doesn't want to talk about it.

SAM: Are you all right?

SHELLEY: Sam, she doesn't want to talk about it.

SAM: Are you all right?

RACHEL: I'm… going to unpack.

SAM: Well, I'm very sorry to hear that.

RACHEL: You know you don't have to pretend anymore. You weren't exactly his biggest fan.

SAM: That's not true.

RACHEL: It is true. I know it. He knows it. I'm going to unpack.

SHELLEY: How long are you staying?

RACHEL: Till the end of the weekend. I have to be back on Monday for a meeting with a new client. They are in so much trouble. And I have to take them through everything because they're going to have to go to court and—

SHELLEY: You should be here for the next week, at least.

RACHEL: The next week?

SAM: Shelley.

SHELLEY: She should be. Shouldn't she?

She looks at SAM.

Dinner will be ready in an hour.

RACHEL: I'm not hungry.

SHELLEY: We told you I'd be making Shabbat dinner.

RACHEL: I know. But my stomach's not doing great.

SHELLEY: Did you eat something to spoil your appetite or—

RACHEL: No. I'm just not feeling very well.

SHELLEY: *(To SAM.)* She needs to eat.

SAM: She'll eat if she wants to eat/

SHELLEY: I wouldn't have made all this food if I had known she wouldn't/

RACHEL: I didn't plan on not feeling well/

SHELLEY: What if you get hungry/

RACHEL: I don't know. I'll have a bagel.

SHELLEY: Rachel! I need those for Temple tomorrow.

SAM: Hey… it's okay.

SHELLEY: You said you wanted to tell her over dinner. You wanted to tell her over dinner, so I made dinner.

RACHEL: Tell me what?

SAM: I'm sure you would have made dinner either way.

SHELLEY: And given the circumstance I thought maybe you'd—

RACHEL: Tell me what?

SAM: You didn't have to go to the trouble of making—

RACHEL: Will one of you tell me what the fuck is going on!

SHELLEY: Rachel, language!

RACHEL: Dad!

SAM and SHELLEY look at each other. Neither wants to respond. After a moment, SHELLEY picks up the knife and starts cutting bagels again. SAM watches her for a moment then turns to RACHEL.

SAM: Rachela… sit.

SAM slowly walks to the couch in the living room. He pats the cushion beside him indicating for her to sit.

Sit.

RACHEL looks at SHELLEY who is trying not to make eye contact with her. RACHEL sits with her father.

RACHEL: What? What is it? You're freaking me out.

SAM: I'm not… well.

RACHEL: Is it your hip or—

SAM: That's part of it. But it's not… I've been having some pain.

SHELLEY: Some pain? Some? He's in pain every day of his life.

SAM: I have been having pain in my hips, my pelvis, my thighs.

SHELLEY: He's in so much pain he can't get out of bed most days. He's exhausted. He's weak. He has no appetite. He—

SAM: We went to see Dr. Powell. He ran some more tests. I've had a relapse. I'm out of remission. It's in my prostate. It's spreading.

RACHEL: Spreading where?

SAM: It's spread to my bones.

RACHEL: Are they going to do more chemo?

SAM: They're not sure.

RACHEL: Not sure of—

SAM: They're not sure how much of a difference it will make.

RACHEL: It made a difference last time.

SAM: It's worse now than last time. Much, much worse.

RACHEL: But you're still going to go through with any kind of treatment they—

SAM: They can't say for certain but... They're giving me a year.

RACHEL: A year to what?

SHELLEY: A year to live!

SAM: If I'm lucky. Likely closer to six months.

SHELLEY: They said six months to a year.

RACHEL: But they're not sure?

SAM: They can't give me any kind of real timeline. But... it's not long.

RACHEL: But it could be. It could be way longer than that. So many people live longer than the time their doctors give them.

SHELLEY: I still think you need a second opinion.

RACHEL: She's right. You do. You absolutely do. You need to talk to someone else about—

SAM: I already know what they're going to say.

RACHEL: How could you possibly know?

SAM: Because I've been to enough appointments over the years and seen enough doctors and had enough tests done to know that—

RACHEL: But things have changed so much since the last time. Things are changing medically every day. I'm sure they'll be able to recommend some other options that—

SAM: Rachel, you don't have many other options at my age.

RACHEL: We should still look into it. I can make some calls. I can—

SHELLEY: It's no use. He's already made up his mind.

RACHEL: Made up his mind not to get a second opinion?

SHELLEY: No. Made up his mind to…

RACHEL: What? To… what?

SAM: I'm… tired.

RACHEL: Do you want to go back to bed?

SAM: It's not that kind of tired. I'm tired everywhere... All over... Every part of me hurts. I can't keep going on like this. I can't-

RACHEL: But chemo would—

SAM: I can't go through all of that again. It was awful. Absolutely awful. I just can't go through it all—

RACHEL: But they can give you something for the pain or the discomfort.

SAM: It's not about… I don't want to feel it. Any of it. I don't want to feel anything.

RACHEL: But there are medications they can give you for the—

SAM: I can't go through with it again.

Beat.

RACHEL: So, what does that mean?

SAM: Well, it means… It means—

SHELLEY: It means your father has decided to kill himself.

Beat.

RACHEL: Is she… serious?

SHELLEY: Your father qualified. There's a doctor here who will do it. He's not very public about it… Even though it's legal he's still very hush-hush about the whole thing. And of course, he isn't Jewish. We couldn't find anyone Jewish who would do it. But he seems very good at all of this. He can have it done here. He doesn't even have to leave his bed if he doesn't want to.

RACHEL: There's a time period, right? Where you have to wait? You can't just do it. You have to wait a certain amount of time to—

SAM: Yes. You have to wait a certain number of weeks—

SHELLEY: Months!

SAM: Before you can move forward.

RACHEL: So, you have time…. You have time still to—

SHELLEY: He's doing it next week. In seven days he'll… He made all the arrangements months ago. We're now past the point of… So, yes… You should tell whoever you have to at work that you're not going to be in the office on Monday or the rest of the week.

RACHEL: You knew… This entire time—

SHELLEY: Of course, I knew.

RACHEL: And you didn't think to tell me?

SHELLEY: It's not as if we talk on a regular basis, now, do we?

RACHEL: You didn't think that maybe something like this would warrant a phone call?

SHELLEY: Would you have picked up if I called?

RACHEL: You told her, but you didn't tell me? You just decide to do this and—

SAM: I didn't just decide. I've been thinking about it for a long time.

RACHEL: How long?

SAM: A while.

RACHEL: How long?

SAM: Years.

RACHEL: You have been thinking about ending your own life for years?

SAM: After the last round I knew that if it ever came back—

RACHEL: And you didn't think to maybe… You have never once said anything about it.

SAM: It's not an easy thing to talk about.

RACHEL: I don't understand how this is even—

SAM: I know this is a lot to take in

RACHEL: Are you sure this isn't something else? Like dementia or Alzheimer's or—

SHELLEY: Rachel, you wish for your father to have Alzheimer's?

RACHEL: Never. But that would at least make more sense. Did you hit your head or have a bad fall that you didn't tell me about? Maybe you have a concussion or… Is this some kind of episode because… This isn't you. This isn't something that you would ever decide to… I don't understand. I don't understand any of this… How you could possibly—

SAM: I want you to be there… when it happens. I want you to—

RACHEL: You can't do this. There has to be some other way. Some other options. I won't let you do this. I won't let you—

SHELLEY shrieks in pain.

SHELLEY: Oww! Oww! Oww! Oww! Oww! Oww! Oww!

SAM: Shell?

SHELLEY: I sliced my hand with the… These stupid bagels! Oww!

SAM gets up from the couch and goes to SHELLEY.

SAM: Let me help.

SHELLEY: Oww!

SAM: Let me help.

RACHEL watches them both in complete disbelief.

Day 2

The next morning.

The main floor of the house is dark.

From offstage the sound of high heels can be heard moving quickly across the floor. Then the sound of someone entering the kitchen. Then the sound of a cupboard being opened, and a kettle being filled with water.

SHELLEY snaps the kitchen lights on. She is very made up in a jacket, skirt, and low heels. Her hand is bandaged.

She sees RACHEL fast asleep at the kitchen table—her head resting on her laptop and still in her clothes from the day before. The contents of her purse are all over the table.

SHELLEY: Rachel.

RACHEL doesn't move.

Rachel!

SHELLEY goes to her and pokes her in the arm. Nothing. She walks right up to her and yells in RACHEL's ear.

(Screaming.) Raaaaaaacheeeeeeeeeel!

RACHEL snaps awake.

RACHEL: What? What is it?

SHELLEY: You were asleep. In your clothes. From yesterday.

RACHEL: And?

SHELLEY: Did you sleep here all night?

RACHEL: I guess. I must have passed out.

She wipes drool from the side of her mouth.

SHELLEY: You look...

RACHEL: You literally just woke me up. What do you look like when you just wake up?

SHELLEY: You should get cleaned up. Brush your hair. Do your face.

RACHEL: Yes, ma'am.

SHELLEY: I am trying to be helpful.

RACHEL: You know what would be helpful… Coffee.

SHELLEY: We're not doing coffee anymore. Only herbal tea.

RACHEL: Since when?

SHELLEY: Since your father's doctor told him he should only be drinking herbal tea.

RACHEL: Well, I need something stronger than that.

SHELLEY: Don't we all.

RACHEL's cell phone rings. She searches for it but can't find it amongst all her stuff. SHELLEY goes to her and hands RACHEL the phone from off the kitchen counter. RACHEL answers it.

RACHEL: *(Into the phone.)* Hi... It's… Yeah. I hope that's okay… It's not good, Darren. It's really not… When?... Today? Why today? You don't have to… If you wait, I can help… It's only been a few weeks. You don't have to… Okay. Okay. If you need me to do anything or… Yeah. Okay, thanks.

She hangs up her phone. She turns around and sees SHELLEY staring at her.

SHELLEY: Everything all right?

RACHEL: Fine.

SHELLEY: How is he?

RACHEL: Who?

SHELLEY: Darren.

RACHEL: He's moving his stuff out of our place today.

SHELLEY: Where will he stay?

RACHEL: At his brother's until we figure out who's going to live where.

SHELLEY: Well, just be thankful you don't own your place together. That could be a nightmare.

RACHEL: Yeah. Right.

Her phone rings again and she answers it.

(Into the phone.) Hi, is everything… He's still asleep, I think… No, why… Why?... What!!!

She grabs her computer and opens it.

(Into the phone.) What time did he… In the morning?... No, I'm looking for it… I said I'm… Oh, no. No, no, no, no, no, no, no.

The landline starts to ring. SHELLEY answers the phone.

SHELLEY: *(Into the phone.)* Hello? Judith, hi!!!

She walks to the living room to take the call. RACHEL reads from her computer screen.

RACHEL: *(Reading.)* "To my dear family and friends, both close and far. There is no easy way to say this, so I'm just going to say it. Because one has so few opportunities in life like this… "

SHELLEY's cell phone starts to ring.

(Reading.) "And I wanted you to hear it from me first."

A cell phone can be heard ringing in another room. Followed by pings and pings of text messages. SHELLEY's cell phone starts pinging with text messages too.

(Reading.) "And I wanted to explain why this is not an easy decision, but why it is the right decision." *(Into the phone.)* Okay, have to go… Come here? You want to come… Darren, are you sure you—

SAM shuffles into the room in his pajamas. He walks with one cane and carries his cell phone in the other hand.

SAM: My phone won't stop ringing.

RACHEL: *(Into the phone.)* He's up. I'll call you back... I said I'll call you back.

She hangs up her cell phone.

Dad! What the fuck is this?

SHELLEY puts her hand over her phone.

SHELLEY: Rachel! For goodness' sake.

RACHEL: What were you thinking?

SHELLEY: Why aren't you dressed?

SAM: We're not leaving for another two hours.

RACHEL: Where are you going?

SHELLEY: To Temple. It's Shabbat. I'm bringing the bagels, remember?

RACHEL: You posted this online? Dad! What were you—

SHELLEY: *(To SAM.)* Judith wants to talk to you.

RACHEL: No. No. No. No, Judith.

SAM: I should say hello—

RACHEL: Can you not be on the phone right now?

SHELLEY: Judith really wants to talk to you.

RACHEL: Who the hell is Judith anyway?

SAM: She's the current president at Temple.

RACHEL: You can call her back.

SAM: What if she needs something or—

RACHEL grabs the phone out of SHELLEY's hand and hangs up.

SHELLEY: I was talking to Judith!

RACHEL: Why would you post this?

SAM: I want people to know. And this felt like the best way to—

RACHEL: You have to take this down. Now! Where's your computer? Get your computer. Or give me your password and I'll take it down for you.

Various phones in the house start ringing. SAM looks at his cell phone in his hand.

No! No, no, no, no, no! Don't answer that.

SAM: It's Joel.

SHELLEY: Joel Hirschmann or Joel Goldman?

SAM: Hirschmann.

SHELLEY: You better get it.

RACHEL: No! No, Joel.

She grabs SAM's cell phone out of his hand. Then grabs SHELLEY's cell phone out of hers.

SHELLEY: Joel is the VP of Finance at Temple. Your father needs to get that.

RACHEL: Joel can wait. Everyone can wait.

SHELLEY: You should never keep Joel waiting. *(To SAM.)* You know he's probably calling to talk to you about Judith.

RACHEL: Did you know he was going to post about this?

SHELLEY: He mentioned that he might.

RACHEL: And you didn't think to stop him?

SHELLEY: I haven't really had much time to think about any of this. It's all happening rather quickly.

The landline rings again. RACHEL walks to the phone and disconnects the cord from the back.

You'll break it!

RACHEL: Why do you even have a landline? No one has a landline anymore.

SHELLEY: We have a landline because people call it.

RACHEL rips the cord out and throws it to the ground.

Rachel!

RACHEL: *(To SHELLEY.)* No! *(To SAM.)* I was up all night... I found dozens of cases where patients were given a prognosis... given a timeline just like you and around your age. And they lived way beyond what their doctors told them. They might be able to treat it. I found an oncologist in Buffalo who—

SHELLEY: Your father can't travel to Buffalo in the state he's in. He can barely get to Temple and it's practically around the corner.

RACHEL: It's a few hours in a car. What's the difference between him sitting here at home or sitting in a vehicle? Look...

RACHEL goes to her computer and turns the screen around to show her father.

They call this guy The Resurrector because he's helped so many people who were told they were going to die. There are tons of articles about him. He's added five, ten, twenty years even to people's lives. He has this whole holistic program that he does.

RACHEL: I sent him an email and left a message and told him all about you and told him that he has to see you—

SAM: T'chiyat hameitim.

RACHEL: What does that mean?

SAM: T'chiyat hameitim. The resurrection of the dead. Most Jewish traditions say that souls can be reincarnated in different bodies if those souls haven't completed their missions on Earth. The Meshiach will come and bring them back to life. But the Mishneh Torah states that the idea that the Meshiach will revive the dead is something only fools believe.

RACHEL: Okay…

SAM: There is no resurrection, Rachel. When you're dead, you're dead.

RACHEL: Dad… I'm talking about an actual human being who could help you. Someone who—

SAM: No one has been able to help me yet. It's been eight years of this.

RACHEL: What if this doctor is different? What if he's actually able to—

SAM: Rachel, there is no magician who can wave a wand and make this go away. I wish there was. It's too late.

RACHEL: But what if it's not?

SAM: This is what happens. We get old. Our bodies get old. And then we—

RACHEL: Bubbie and Zadie both lived into their nineties.

SHELLEY: Didn't your father die in his eighties?

SAM: He was eighty-eight.

RACHEL: I'm just saying they lived a long life. You have good genes.

SAM: Apparently, I don't.

SHELLEY: She's trying to lawyer you, Sam. Don't listen to her.

RACHEL: What I'm trying to do is show you that there's another way. Can't you at least give this guy a chance? Can't we at least go and see if he can actually—

SAM: Rachel… No.

RACHEL: Then I'll find someone who's closer. How long can you be in the car? What, an hour at the most?

SAM: It's not about the car.

RACHEL: I'll do some more research. There has to be someone who—

Suddenly, RACHEL is struck by a wave of nausea. Then dizziness. She grabs hold of a nearby chair.

SHELLEY: Rachel, listen to what he's saying. Your father said no.

RACHEL: I… I think I'm going to be sick.

SHELLEY: Now?

RACHEL rushes to the kitchen sink and leans over.

Grab her hair.

SAM: Her hair?

SHELLEY: So, she doesn't… Grab her hair.

SAM slowly moves to RACHEL, but she motions that she needs space. She holds her own hair back and starts dry heaving.

Now, I'm going to be sick. I can't hear someone… without it making me… Oh god…

She covers her mouth. RACHEL coughs into the sink.

I need the bathroom.

As she runs to the bathroom offstage RACHEL dry heaves into the sink.

SAM: Oy.

Day 3

The next day.

The main floor is empty. The doorbell to the house rings. RACHEL rushes to open the front door and finds ELI. He's dressed in pants, a collared shirt, a sweater over top, and a kippah.

ELI: Rachel. Hello.

RACHEL: Hi. Thank you so much for coming.

ELI: Of course.

RACHEL: I didn't know who else to call or… I thought you of all people might be able to talk some sense into him. I didn't pull you away from services or—

ELI: No. No services today.

RACHEL: Okay. Good. It's nice to see you despite the…

ELI: Despite the circumstance, yes. You're all grown up.

RACHEL: I know. I don't know how it happened, but it did. I can't even remember the last time I saw you.

ELI: Joshua's bar mitzvah.

RACHEL: Wow. Yeah, I guess it was. How is he? How are the girls?

ELI: Everyone is good… healthy. Your father tells me you're well... that everything at work is good. You're a hotshot lawyer in the big city. He's very proud of you. He talks about you all the time. You know… He never sounds happier than when he's talking about you.

RACHEL: That's really… Thanks. Thanks for saying that.

ELI: How's the boyfriend?

RACHEL: He's not… my boyfriend. We're not together anymore. We broke up.

ELI: Oh. Well, I hope that feels like a good decision.

RACHEL: I don't know what kind of decision it feels like. We want different things. He wants to get married… have a family.

ELI: Oy. And you don't?

RACHEL: I don't know. We barely see each other anymore. He works nights. And I just started at this new firm and the hours are long and—

ELI: You know, Rachel… Love is very important.

RACHEL: Yes. I know.

ELI: Love will be what gets you through the darkest days and the coldest winters. We need love. All of us do.

RACHEL: I know. We just—

SAM: *(Offstage.)* Rachel? Who are you talking to?

RACHEL: He doesn't know I asked you to come.

ELI: You thought you would catch your father off guard? Do you know who you're dealing with?

RACHEL: Yeah. I do.

SAM shuffles into the room, now using a cane in each hand.

Dad! Rabbi Limmer… I don't even know what to call you.

ELI: Eli.

RACHEL: Eli just stopped by.

SAM: Stopped by?

RACHEL: Yeah. He was in the area.

SAM: In the area?

ELI: Yeah. In the area.

SAM: What were you doing in the area?

RACHEL: He was getting some groceries and—

SAM: She called you, didn't she?

ELI: She called me, yes.

RACHEL: No. I didn't. He was driving by and he—

SAM: You know… If you lie about a rabbi you immediately go to hell

RACHEL: What?

SAM: If you lie about a rabbi you go to hell and your soul burns for all of eternity.

RACHEL: *(To ELI.)* Is that true?

ELI: No. It's not true.

RACHEL: Dad! Don't do that.

SAM: Rachel, it's fine. We need to talk anyway.

RACHEL: Okay. I'm going to do some work. If you need anything I'll be downstairs—

SAM: We'll be fine.

RACHEL: Okay. But if you do—

SAM: We'll be fine.

RACHEL looks at them and then leaves. SAM and ELI look at each other for a moment alone.

So?

ELI: So.

SAM: You look good.

ELI: I'm trying to eat better. Laying off the chips after dinner.

SAM: It's working.

ELI: Thanks.

SAM: And me?

ELI: You? You look like garbage.

SAM: I feel like garbage. Can I get you anything? I'm going to have something. What do you want? Water? Tea? A Scotch? I think we have a bottle of Dr. Brown's.

ELI: What kind of Dr. Brown's?

SAM: Root beer.

ELI: If it's not the Black Cherry, why bother?

SAM: You know how hard it is to find Dr. Brown's Black Cherry Soda?

ELI: Well, if Johnston's was still open—

SAM: Johnston's! I haven't thought about that place in years.

ELI: I think about it every time I want a Black Cherry soda. Nothing for me though.

SAM heads for the kitchen but struggles to move.

Do you want me to get you something?

SAM: You know what… I'm not really thirsty. Here. Sit, sit.

He slowly makes his way over to a chair near ELI.

I was going to call you.

ELI: But you didn't.

SAM: You didn't either. It's a funny thing, huh? Talking about all of this.

ELI: You seemed fine to talk about it online.

SAM: Ah. You saw that.

ELI: I think everyone who knows you saw that.

The landline rings.

SHELLEY: *(Offstage.)* Sam!

SAM: *(Calling back.)* I know. It's fine, Shell. Just let it—

SHELLEY answers the phone offstage.

SHELLEY: *(Offstage.)* Hello?

SAM: Our phones have been ringing off the hook. Think I've talked to more people in the last twenty-four hours than I have in the last twenty-four years. Susan Abrams called and talked my ear off for an hour and a half. I can't remember the last time I spoke to Susan. Michael Brenner called. Elliot Schachter, Henry Berkowitz—

ELI: What you've decided to do, it's… it's shaken people. My phone's been ringing off the hook too. People are calling me, emailing me, texting me.

SAM: You? What do they want with you?

ELI: People are asking for support. They want answers. How can he do something like this? How can he even contemplate something like this? Isn't it so un-Jewish? You mean a lot to a lot of people here. You're a vital member of the Jewish community in this city.

SAM: I don't know how vital I am.

ELI: Please… Past president of our Temple. You led the building of our education centre. You've organized every major fundraiser we've had in the last decade. You donate to every major Jewish cause in the country.

ELI: You've done free legal work for countless Jewish organizations. You head our multicultural committee. You're the reason the Temple has a new ark for the Torah. You perform at every Temple talent show—

SAM: Yeah, yeah, yeah. You've seen my resume.

ELI: I know you. And others do too. And even if they don't know you they feel like they do. You're someone who gets things done… Someone who's there for other people… Someone who's selfless, and kind, and…

Beat.

People are having a lot of trouble processing this… All of this. Because if you are prepared to do something like this… What does that say about them? Huh? What does that say about us? This news of yours… You know…

Beat.

When you first told me you that you were going to see if you qualified for… I thought it was something you were looking into… Theoretically, speaking. I never thought it was something you would actually go ahead and—

SHELLEY: *(Offstage.)* Sam, the Rosenburgs want to talk to you.

SAM: *(Calling back.)* Tell them I'll call them tomorrow.

SHELLEY: *(Offstage.)* Are you sure?

SAM: *(Calling back.)* Yes.

SHELLEY: *(Offstage.)* He'll call you in an hour.

SAM: Oy, what's the point?

ELI: Sam… I don't know if I should be talking to you as your rabbi or as one of your oldest friends.

SAM: It's your choice.

Beat.

ELI: You know what… I'll have that Scotch.

SAM starts to get up to get a drink.

Don't move. I'll get it. I know where it is.

ELI goes to a cabinet in the living room.

You want one?

SAM: I'm not allowed.

ELI: Come on. Have one.

SAM: I'm not supposed to drink.

ELI takes out two glasses and pours them each a drink.

ELI: You're breaking the biggest rule of them all. Why start obeying them now, right?

ELI holds up his glass.

ELI: L'chaim.

Beat.

Can I even say that in this situation?

SAM: You can say whatever you like. I know you're going to anyway.

ELI: I'm trying very hard not to.

SAM: Eli—

ELI: It's murder, Sam. Plain and simple. What you are talking about doing… It's murder.

SAM: Things are progressing in the world, you know.

ELI: Yes. I do know. It's legal here. And it's becoming more and more popular by the day but… For us… For Jews… It's murder.

SAM: That's progressing too. And you know it. This is the direction we are moving in—

ELI: There's no "we" here. This is the direction you are moving in. For me…as someone who devotes every waking moment to our people… in here *(He points to his heart.)*… and up here *(He points to his head.)*… it's murder. You are committing murder against yourself. And this random doctor that you found to—

SAM: Eli, he's not random. He's at University Hospital. He's one of the best doctors they have.

ELI: Yeah? Well, he'll be committing murder too. And that… all of that will be on you. On you and your conscience because you have decided to do this.

SAM: He's doing this freely. Of his own free will. I'm not forcing him to do—

ELI: Lo Tirzach. Lo Tirzach. Thou shalt not murder. It's a commandment. It is *the* commandment.

SAM: Eli, we're Reform. The rules are… open to interpretation. Or they should be.

ELI: Around some things... sure. But this... It doesn't matter what branch of Judaism you follow—Reform, Orthodox, Conservative... Murder is murder. And you can't escape that.

SAM: There are countless stories of Jews doing this now. Reform Jews making this decision. Reform rabbis supporting their congregants when they're making these decisions—

ELI: Well, I'm not one of them. It would be no different than you inviting me over here to plot another man's death. Only instead of talking about killing someone else, we're talking about killing you.

SAM: So, what am I supposed to do?

ELI: Don't do it. Don't do this. That's what you do.

Beat.

SAM: I want you to be in the room. As my rabbi. As my friend—

ELI: Oy. Sam—

SAM: I know it's asking a lot. But I need you there. If anyone is going to say any kind of blessing... I want it to be you. I don't want to ask some rabbi that I don't know to—

ELI: Good luck finding a rabbi here who would even—

SAM: There are doctors. There are rabbis. There are people who will do this. But I want it to be you.

Beat.

ELI: I have known you longer than anyone else in my life.

SAM: What about your mother? Your sister? How is she, by the way?

ELI: She's pissed.

SAM: At who?

ELI: At you.

SAM: How does she know?

ELI: She follows you on Facebook.

SAM: Right. I keep forgetting about that.

ELI: Other than my family… I have known you longer than anyone else in my life. You are the closest thing I have to a brother.

SAM: My apologies. You deserve better.

Beat.

ELI: Benjamin Bloom. Sixth grade. Benjamin Bloom.

SAM: Oy, not this story.

ELI: Benjamin Bloom had been making his rounds in our class and decided to choose me to pick on that week.

SAM: Pick on? No, he was shoving you into walls.

ELI: And you and I were sitting on the curb trading baseball cards. He came waltzing over with his two sideyucks. Said something about stealing my lunch money. And you told him to go away. He looked at you like his head was going to spin all the way around his body. You told him again. And when he wouldn't move, what did you do?

SAM: I did what anyone would have done in that situation. I leaned forward and punched him in the balls/

ELI: You leaned forward, and you punched him in the balls. And that's how Benjamin Bloom became…

SAM/ELI: Benny Ballsack.

ELI: That's the kind of person you were. Willing to punch someone else in the balls for your friends and family. You were good. You are good. You're a good person, Sam. We're supposed to grow old together. Live in the same retirement home… Trading cards on the curb together.

SAM: You know how long it would take me to get up from the curb now? You're lucky your health has been good, Eli.

ELI: B'ezrat HaShem.

SAM: B'ezrat HaShem, yes. We're not all that lucky.

So, if I do this… I'm what? I'm not good anymore… Is that what you're saying?

ELI: Well… If I don't do this, then I'm what? I'm not a good rabbi? Is that what you're saying?

SAM: If I was just another member of our Temple asking you to—

ELI: If you were another member of our Temple I would have left by now. What you're asking me to do... to be there for you… like this... as a friend… as a rabbi it's…

Beat.

SAM: Well, while you're mulling that over… I need something else.

ELI: Something else? Oy, what now? You're breaking my heart.

SAM: I need you to officiate my wedding.

He reaches into his pocket and pulls out a small box.

ELI: Does she know?

SAM: She has no idea.

ELI: Well, you better tell her soon, don't you think?

SHELLEY enters the room, dressed to run errands.

SHELLEY: The Rosenburgs are expecting your call. I'm going to run out to grab some groceries for dinner. Is there anything you want me to—

She stops in her tracks when she sees the box in his hand.

What is that?

SAM: What is what?

SHELLEY: That box. What is that?

SAM: Oh, this?

SHELLEY: Don't tease me, Samuel Adelman. *(To ELI.)* Hi, Eli.

ELI: Hi, Shelley.

SHELLEY: Well?

SAM looks at her and holds out his hand.

SAM: Come here.

SHELLEY goes to him. SAM opens the box and presents her with the ring.

Shelley Sarah Hoffman… Will you marry me?

SHELLEY screams with delight and instantly starts to cry.

SHELLEY: Yes! Of course. Of course, I'll marry you!

SHELLEY kisses him on the lips. Then plants kisses all over his face. He takes her finger and slides the ring on. She looks at it, beaming from ear to ear.

I thought you didn't want to get married.

SAM: Turns out I do.

SHELLEY: But are we going to have a wedding? When are we possibly going to—

SAM: How long would it take you to find a dress?

SHELLEY: I don't know. I could probably find something in the next day or two.

SAM: *(To ELI.)* Are you free in two days?

ELI: I'll see what I can do.

SAM: Then we're getting married in two days.

SHELLEY: Are you sure sure? With everything that's going on, does this even make sense to—

SAM: Shelley… I'm sure.

SAM slides the ring on her finger. SHELLEY screams at the top of her lungs and hugs him. As she does, RACHEL enters the room.

RACHEL: Did you do it? Did you get him to change his—

SHELLEY holds out her hand.

SHELLEY: We're getting married! Me and your father… We're getting—

RACHEL: What!

SHELLEY hugs SAM and squeals with delight.

Day 4

The next afternoon.

The main floor of the house is empty. From offstage we hear the sound of people kicking off their shoes. SHELLEY comes into the living room, carrying what looks like hundreds of shopping and garment bags.

SHELLEY: Bring them in here.

RACHEL comes into the living room also carrying a ton of shopping bags.

RACHEL: We couldn't have done this at the mall?

SHELLEY: I couldn't handle your complaining—

RACHEL: I wasn't complaining—

SHELLEY: I was dragging you from store to store. You were a complete and utter pain in the tuchus the entire time. I figured it was better to buy everything and come back here to try things—

RACHEL: I just don't think we should be wasting our time shopping when—

SHELLEY: We are not wasting our time, Rachel. We are looking for a dress for you for my wedding.

She pulls out a bag and hands it to RACHEL.

SHELLEY: Here. Try this one.

RACHEL: This one? Really?

SHELLEY: Go.

RACHEL goes to the bathroom offstage to try on the dress.

(Calling to her.) I want to see it on you whether you like it or not.

She starts to organize the other bags.

RACHEL: *(Offstage.)* Oh my god.

SHELLEY: *(Calling to her.)* What?

RACHEL: *(Offstage.)* This thing takes up the entire bathroom.

SHELLEY: *(Calling to her.)* I want to see it.

RACHEL: *(Offstage.)* I can't get it done up.

SHELLEY: *(Calling to her.)* Then I'll do it up for you.

RACHEL comes out of the bathroom in a bright pink dress with ruffles on the sleeve. The skirt is so large RACHEL has trouble getting through the bathroom door.

Come here.

RACHEL: No.

SHELLEY: Come.

RACHEL goes to her.

RACHEL: It's too tight. It's not going to zip up.

SHELLEY: Suck your stomach in.

RACHEL: I am.

SHELLEY: Suck it in.

RACHEL: I am.

SHELLEY: If you lost a few pounds this might actually—

RACHEL: Shelley!

SHELLEY does up the zipper on the dress.

SHELLEY: There. What do you think?

RACHEL: I look like I'm wearing a pink garbage bag… with frills.

SHELLEY: Well, I like it.

RACHEL: You like this?

SHELLEY: Yes.

RACHEL: I look like someone splattered Pepto Bismol all over/

SHELLEY: Fine. Fine. Try this!

She pulls out another bag and hands it to RACHEL. As RACHEL heads back to the bathroom…

Wait!

SHELLEY undoes the zipper on the dress and RACHEL leaves for the bathroom.

RACHEL: Are you sure you wouldn't rather have one of your friends be your maid of honour? Like your best friend maybe?

SHELLEY: Your father is my best friend. And I can't exactly have the groom as my maid of honour.

RACHEL: There isn't anyone else you want to ask?

She comes out of the bathroom in another dress with ruffles on the sleeve and a large skirt. It looks similar to the other dress only it's a peach, salmon, coral sort of colour.

I don't even know what colour this is.

SHELLEY: It looks nice with your skin tone.

RACHEL: Is this from the same store as the last one?

SHELLEY: No.

RACHEL: More than one store makes dresses like this?

SHELLEY: It's a popular style.

RACHEL: From what decade?

SHELLEY pulls down the sleeves and adjusts the skirt.

SHELLEY: And it was your father's idea… by the way.

RACHEL: What was his idea?

SHELLEY: That I ask you to be my maid of honour. It wasn't my idea.

RACHEL: Awesome.

SHELLEY starts to play with RACHEL's hair.

SHELLEY: This looks nice on you. This could work if you had your hair up and a bold lip.

RACHEL: Please don't make me wear this.

SHELLEY: Do you want to try on another one then?

RACHEL: Is it better than the last two?

SHELLEY hands her another bag with a dress to try on.

SHELLEY: Here.

RACHEL takes it to the bathroom. On her way there she trips on the skirt of the dress she is wearing.

RACHEL: You see? I can't wear this. I'm going to end up breaking my neck.

SHELLEY: With the right shoes—

RACHEL: Shoes. Fuck. I forgot about shoes.

SHELLEY: Rachel. Language. And you have to wear shoes. It's a wedding.

I'm not going to let you walk around barefoot or in socks—

RACHEL: Shelley, I'm not going to wear socks to your wedding. Don't worry. I can't wait to see what hideous footwear you've chosen for me to wear—

SHELLEY: Why can't you just be happy for me?

RACHEL: I am. I'm happy for you.

SHELLEY: Then why haven't you congratulated me?

RACHEL: Congratulations.

SHELLEY: Why haven't you congratulated me without having to be prompted?

RACHEL: There hasn't been time.

SHELLEY: You've had plenty of time to—

RACHEL: Why don't I try on this dress?

SHELLEY: You don't want us to get married? You don't want me to marry your father, is that it?

RACHEL: It's part of it—

SHELLEY: Because you don't want me to be your mother?

RACHEL: My mother?

SHELLEY: Technically… moving forward… I will be your mother. Yes—

RACHEL: No. No, no, no, no, no. Not technically.

SHELLEY: And you probably feel like I'm trying to replace her but—

RACHEL: My mother died almost twenty years ago, Shelley. You're not replacing anyone.

SHELLEY: Because I don't want to be your mother. I want us to be—

RACHEL: This is insane. This is completely—

SHELLEY: What, Rachel? What is—

RACHEL: This… All of this. It's insane. It's insane that you are marrying my dad days before he's ending his own life. It's fucking insane. And I know, I know… Language. You're always on me about my fucking language. You're on me all the time… About absolutely everything. And you want me to be happy for you? This is all for Dad. All of it. This wedding. This—

SHELLEY: You just don't like the idea of marriage. You are one of those women who live in their own little feminist bubble/

RACHEL: Excuse me/

SHELLEY: Where you judge every woman around you for wanting a life that is different than yours. For wanting a life that they actually/

RACHEL: I don't care what you want with your life. After Dad's gone, we're never going to see each other again. And as long as you don't screw him over—

Beat.

SHELLEY: How would I possibly screw over your father?

RACHEL: How?

SHELLEY: Yes. How?

RACHEL: Well… My dad wasn't in good shape when the two of you met.

SHELLEY: And?

RACHEL: And he certainly hasn't gotten better since the two of you have been together.

SHELLEY: And?

RACHEL: And he was probably very honest with you about his financial situation. That he's done extremely well for himself over the years.

SHELLEY: And?

RACHEL: And I get it. You put in a few years with this older guy who's likely to not make it very long and leave with your head held high.

SHELLEY: That's what you think? That's what you think of me? That all these years I've just been waiting for him to die so that I can take his money?

RACHEL: How could I not think that?

SHELLEY: Easily. There are hundreds of other things you could think about regarding me and your—

RACHEL: Well, I am sure you would think the exact same thing if—

SHELLEY: I wouldn't,actually. I would never think something like that. Especially because I have made it abundantly clear over the years that I love your father... that I am completely and utterly devoted to him. I had waited for years for someone like Sam to come along… years. I was engaged. I had a lineup of men waiting to propose. And it didn't work out with any of them. You want to know why? Because they weren't Sam. Yes, there is an age difference between us. I know that. He knows that. We can both count. And you're right… your father hasn't been well… and he's only gotten worse in the time we've been together. You're absolutely right. But who has been the one taking care of him all these years? Who is the one that has committed themselves to making sure that every moment of his life is—

RACHEL: Shelley, I help however I can.

SHELLEY: Rachel, you don't live here. There is only so much that you can do.

RACHEL: I've offered to move back so I can help. I offered to help him with work. Dad wouldn't let me—

SHELLEY: Because your life and your job aren't here.

RACHEL: I've still done whatever I can to—

SHELLEY: But I'm the one who is here, Rachel. Me. I'm the one who drives him to his doctor's appointments. I'm the one who takes notes during those appointments so that your father has all the information he needs when we get home. I'm the one who nursed him back to health after both of his surgeries. I'm the one who makes sure he does his exercises. I'm the one who makes sure he takes his medication. I feed him. I bathe him. I get him out of bed every morning. I get him dressed. I tuck him into bed every night. I even wipe his ass after he's gone to the bathroom if he needs it. And I do all of that gladly because I love your father. And when all of this is over… after he's… I will continue to love your father until the day I—

RACHEL: Then how can you let him do this? How can you possibly let him go through with this? If you love him… if you actually really love him—

SHELLEY: You think I haven't tried everything in my power to change your father's mind? You know him. Your father is a wonderful man, Rachel… A wonderful, brilliant, wilfully stubborn man. And once he has made up his mind to do something… there is no changing it. You know that. I know that. He made his choice... regardless of how we feel about it. And now we all have to live with it.

RACHEL: And what if I don't know how to?

SHELLEY: What do you want me to say? I don't have any answers for you, Rachel. You are not the only one losing someone you love. I am losing the love of my life. I'm losing—

The doorbell rings. SHELLEY and RACHEL look at each other. SHELLEY goes to the front door and finds DARREN. He's wearing street clothes and carries a duffle bag.

DARREN: Hi.

RACHEL: Hi.

SHELLEY: What is he doing here?

DARREN: Should I go or—

RACHEL: No.

SHELLEY: You didn't tell me he was coming.

RACHEL: I didn't know he was coming.

DARREN: Rach, I asked you if you wanted me to come. I asked you if—

RACHEL: I know. But I didn't think you would actually—

DARREN: I asked you over the phone. I texted you, like, five times whether you wanted me to come or—

RACHEL: I know. I just—

DARREN: I wouldn't have driven two and a half hours if you didn't actually want me to—

RACHEL: I know. I do. I just didn't think you would actually show up.

DARREN: Well… I did.

RACHEL looks at SHELLEY.

RACHEL: Can we have a minute?

SHELLEY: No. The mall closes in an hour.

DARREN: The mall?

SHELLEY: If you won't wear any of these then we have to go back to the mall and find something that you'll actually—

RACHEL: Shelley, just give us a minute… Please.

SHELLEY: Fine. Fine. But I'm timing you.

RACHEL: Okay.

SHELLEY: And close the door. You're going to let all the warm air out.

She storms off as DARREN closes the door behind him. RACHEL and DARREN look at each other.

RACHEL: Hi.

DARREN: Hi.

RACHEL: You're here.

DARREN: I am. I don't have to be.

RACHEL: No. No. I just… It's good to see you.

DARREN: Yeah. You too. Nice dress.

RACHEL: Stop.

DARREN: It's nice. You look nice.

RACHEL: What every woman always wants to hear... You look nice.

DARREN: You look beautiful. Come here.

Out of habit DARREN reaches to hug her. RACHEL takes a step back.

Sorry. I—

RACHEL: No. I'm just not sure if we're... Are we hugging? I'm not sure what we're allowed to—

DARREN: You think the hug police are going to come to the front door and—

RACHEL: We haven't seen each other face-to-face in a few weeks and—

DARREN: Three. Three weeks.

RACHEL: Right. I just want to make sure that it's okay to hug each other and... You hate the drive here.

DARREN: I do.

RACHEL: And you still came.

DARREN: I did.

RACHEL: Darren...

SHELLEY bursts back into the room.

SHELLEY: Timer's off.

RACHEL goes to sit down.

Rachel, don't smush the dress.

RACHEL: Let it smush. I don't care.

DARREN: That's a lot of ruffles. I kind of like it.

SHELLEY: You see!

RACHEL: You are not allowed to like this.

SHELLEY: There's more. Do you want to see the others?

DARREN: Sure.

SHELLEY hands RACHEL another dress to try on.

RACHEL: Don't make me do it.

SHELLEY: Go!

RACHEL drags herself into the bathroom with another dress.

DARREN: Mazel tov, by the way.

SHELLEY: Finally! Thank you, Darren. Thank you for saying that.

DARREN: I mean it. I think it's really lovely you're doing this.

SHELLEY: Me too.

DARREN: How are you?

SHELLEY: Oh, I am just fine.

DARREN: Yeah. How are you really?

SHELLEY: Oh, I'm a fucking mess.

Day 4

Later that evening.

The main floor of the house is dark.

From offstage the sound of slippers shuffling across the floor can be heard. Then the sound of someone entering the kitchen. Then light streams into the room as the freezer door is opened. SAM pulls out a tub of ice cream. SAM turns on the kitchen light.

He is in his pajamas, and slippers, and walks with one cane. As he goes to grab a spoon, he sees DARREN sitting at the kitchen table. The sight of him nearly causes him to have a heart attack.

SAM: Oy gevalt. You almost scared me to death. I didn't know you were coming. When did you get here?

DARREN: A few hours ago. You've been asleep.

SAM: I usually am. Are you always in the habit of sitting in the dark at this hour?

DARREN: Are you always in the habit of sneaking ice cream at this hour?

SAM: If you must know… Yes. I'm going to watch a game and eat this entire tub.

DARREN: I'm usually playing a show at this time.

SAM: Yes. That's right. The deejaying.

DARREN: Yes. The deejaying.

Beat.

SAM: Okay. Enjoy the rest of your night.

He turns to leave.

DARREN: That's it? You're going to walk away? Just like that?

SAM: I have a game to watch.

DARREN: You must have been pretty happy, huh?

SAM: Happy about what?

DARREN: About me and Rachel… about us breaking up. I know she told you. She tells you everything.

SAM: She told me. Though she didn't say much about it.

DARREN: No? Usually she tells you every little detail about everything in her—

SAM: Well, she hasn't. Not about this. And I wasn't happy. I was… surprised.

DARREN: Surprised?

SAM: You'd been together for a while.

DARREN: Seven years.

SAM: So, I was… surprised.

DARREN: Oh, please. You must have been over the fucking moon.

SAM: You know what… suddenly I've lost my appetite.

He puts the ice cream back in the freezer.

DARREN: You know… I came here for Rachel. Obviously. Someone shouldn't have to go through something like this alone.

SAM: I agree with that.

DARREN: But really… I came to see you.

SAM: Me?

DARREN: Sam, I've been doing a lot of work on myself lately. Trying to work through some things. Trying to put good things out into the universe in the hopes that they will come back in some way.

SAM: Uh-huh.

DARREN: And I thought that since you are going to... That since you're going to... I can't even say it.

SAM: Since I am going to end my own life?

DARREN: Since you're going to end your own life, yes... I thought that we should talk. That we should finally talk. That we should resolve our differences, once and for all.

SAM: I don't think there's anything to—

DARREN: You don't like me. And I've never come and talked to you about it. I admit that. That's on me. But I never wanted to get between you and Rachel... or make things worse between you and me because... you are so important to her. You know that. You must know that. Your word is like the word of God to Rachel. And that's hard to compete with. It's been hard. It's been really hard. And I don't know what I've done or said over the years that's made you so—

SAM: You haven't done anything.

DARREN: So, I said something that—

SAM: No.

DARREN: Then... What? I know you never wanted me and Rachel to be together. I know you didn't want us to get married.

SAM: I never said that I—

DARREN: But you've never wanted us to be together. I can't stop thinking about the fact that maybe... that maybe if you were even a little bit more supportive of our relationship... that Rachel and I might still be together.

SAM: I see.

DARREN: Sam… In all the time that Rachel and I were dating you and I never spent any time together… just us… alone. Not once. That's weird. To me that's weird.

SAM: That's not so weird.

DARREN: It's weird, Sam.

SAM: Well… You don't like sports.

DARREN: Okay. But you like a lot of other stuff. You talk to other people about a lot of other stuff. I've seen you talk to people about all kinds of subjects. But you never asked me about work or my family or me... ever. You never took any kind of interest in me. And I know way too much about you because Rachel talks about you all the freaking time but also… because I ask. I ask how you are, how work is, what's going on at the synagogue… Meanwhile, you've just been waiting for her to get rid of me and—

SAM: I have not been waiting for her to get rid of—

DARREN: Is it because I'm not Jewish? Is that it?

SAM: Well, that certainly wouldn't hurt.

DARREN: Because honestly, at this point… I'm more Jewish than Rachel is. I go to every High Holiday service. I celebrate every major holiday and festival. I told her we should start having Shabbat dinner every Friday night together… invite friends over… invite you two over and make a thing of it.

DARREN: I found challah recipes so we could make our own loaves from scratch. I researched how we could set up a sukkah on our condo balcony so we could celebrate together. Rachel didn't want to... She thought I was crazy. But if she had said yes... I would have set it up in a heartbeat. Rachel doesn't even know when Purim is. I do. I know when Purim is. I've done so much work and spent so much time trying to take an interest in all of this... for Rachel, yes. But also... mainly... for you. So you'll ease up and maybe look me in the eye every once in a while or show any signs of giving a damn that I'm in the same room as you.

SAM: Darren—

DARREN: I have always been good to her. I have always put her first.

SAM: Being good to her is not enough. You can't... Never mind.

DARREN: What? I can't... What? You're not going to get many other chances to say this so you might as well just—

SAM: You can't take care of her.

Beat.

DARREN: Okay... So... I'm not sure if you know this but Rachel is more than capable of taking care of herself.

SAM: I know you think that. And I know she thinks that. But what if something happens?

DARREN: I would never let anything happen to her. I would do everything in my power to make sure nothing will ever—

SAM: Something will happen. Something always happens. Pain will always find a way to your doorstep. It's unavoidable. And I want to know that she'll be taken care of.

DARREN: Like, financially or—

SAM: Financially. Emotionally. Spiritually. I want her taken care of in every way possible.

Beat.

For years it was always just us. Me and Rachela. We were a team. She was never the same after her mother died. You want to talk about hard… That was hard. It was impossibly hard. She was so close to her mother. She loved her so so much. After she died, and it was just the two of us… I tried to love Rachel more than any father could possibly love their daughter. I wanted Rachel to feel as if she had a hundred fathers who would do anything for her. Even though it was only us. Rachel was my everything. And I have tried to give her the best life possible—

DARREN: You have. No one is saying you didn't give her a good life—

SAM: But now… I can't go unless I know that she's going to be all right.

Because I won't be there to…

Beat.

When she was little... This started around when she was four... She had the sweetest, smallest face with these short bangs... I would call the house when I was leaving the office for the day on my way home. I'd call and talk to Barbara... Rachel's mother... and then she'd put Rachel on the phone, and I would sing to her.

He sings a few lines of the chorus of the song "I Just Called to Say I Love You." Then looks at DARREN.

It's a Stevie Wonder song.

DARREN: Yeah, I know who sings it, Sam. Everyone knows who sings it.

SAM: Well, when she got old enough, we started singing it together. And when she was old enough to have her own phone, I would call her, and I'd sing it. And then I'd leave messages for her when she was away at university, and I'd sing it. And even since then, when she's working a big case and or has some big life event where I know she needs some extra love... I call her up and I sing it to her. And to this day... every time I do... all I hear... all I see... is her little face and those little bangs and the way she said my name when I called her.

DARREN: Sam, she's not a little girl anymore.

SAM: See? That's where you are wrong. She will always, always be my little girl.

Beat.

DARREN: My dad died when I was a kid. Did you know that?

SAM: I think I knew that.

DARREN: You think?

SAM: I'm sure I knew that at some point, yes.

DARREN: I was four. He was in a car accident. Hit by a drunk driver. My dad never had a drink in his entire life. And my mom raised me and my two brothers all by herself. So, if we're talking about hard… I get it. I really do. We're all just trying to carry on the best we can. That's all we can do.

SAM stares at him. Then he opens the freezer and pulls out the ice cream tub. He goes to get two spoons and slowly makes his way over to the table. He sits down, opens the tub, and scoops out a spoonful. He passes a spoon down towards DARREN. Then sends the ice cream tub in his direction.

Aren't you going to miss this?

SAM: What? Miss ice cream? You betcha. Why do you think I'm up at this hour shoving my face with spoonfuls of it?

DARREN: I don't just mean this. Aren't you going to miss… everything?

SAM: I'll miss some things. But some other things… not so much. Pass that back.

DARREN sends the tub back towards SAM.

DARREN: You're really going to do this?

SAM: I go back and forth on it. One minute I'm certain. The next minute it feels like the biggest mistake I could make. Then my body aches and I feel like giving up and I'm certain all over again. It's a bit of a seesaw in my head, really.

Beat.

What do you think I should do?

SAM sends the tub towards DARREN.

DARREN: Me?

SAM: You're saying I don't ask you anything. I'm asking. What do you think I should do?

DARREN: I think it's your decision.

SAM: You're not going to try and talk me out of it?

DARREN: I'm pretty sure everyone else is already trying to do that.

SAM: Yes. Yes, they are.

DARREN: If I was in the kind of pain that you're in... and for so long... I'd probably do the same thing.

Beat.

I was going to propose, you know... to Rachel.

SAM: And?

DARREN: And she doesn't want to get married.

SAM: But you want to marry her?

DARREN: Of course, I want to marry her. I'd marry Rachel tomorrow if I could.

SAM: Tomorrow is my wedding day. I won't have you upstaging me.

DARREN: I love weddings.

SAM: Who doesn't?

DARREN: Other than your daughter?

SAM: Other than my daughter, yes.

DARREN: Why? Why is she like that?

SAM: She doesn't like change.

DARREN: Even the good ones?

SAM: Sometimes even the good ones. Give it.

DARREN smiles then sends the tub back to SAM.

SAM: What about work?

DARREN: What about it?

SAM: What will you do about work?

DARREN: I have a job.

SAM: The deejaying?

DARREN: Yes.

SAM: That's not work.

DARREN: Yes. It is.

SAM: You can't be deejaying at some club at my age.

DARREN: I'm a really big deal. Do you know that? I have thousands and thousands of followers.

SAM: You're not helping your cause, Darren.

DARREN: I'm booked every week. I'm booked up for the next three years.

I'm literally supposed to be playing a show right now. And I make a really decent living from it.

SAM: Uh-huh.

DARREN: I get that I'm not a doctor or a lawyer or whatever other profession qualifies for you. But I am really successful. Just because you don't understand that world or that success doesn't mean I'm not. I'm good at what I do.

SAM: Do you have any savings?

DARREN: Some.

SAM: Enough to buy a house?

DARREN: No one has enough to buy a house right now.

SAM: If you were a doctor or a lawyer…

DARREN: If I was a doctor or a lawyer I'd still be paying off my student debt. Not everyone had the kind of help Rachel had. Plus, I'd never see Rachel… or my kids.

SAM: You can't see Rachel and the kids if you're deejaying every night.

DARREN: That's why I work construction during the day to—

SAM: Yes, you have hundreds of jobs. I lose count.

DARREN: A lot of people we know have more than one job right now, Sam. It's just a part of life. Everyone is hustling. Everyone is trying to get by. I know you were this insanely successful lawyer and climbed the ladder super quick.

DARREN: But things are different. And it is so expensive to be alive right now. So yes… I might not be able to buy a house… like, right at this exact moment… but I will. And… I can work on a house. I know how to fix things. I know how to make things better. Rachel says every time something went wrong at home you had to open the phone book and call someone to fix it.

SAM: I can fix things.

DARREN: Uh-huh.

SAM: I can. Jews are great with their hands. We built the pyramids in Egypt.

DARREN: Yeah, not by choice. I work hard. I will never not work hard. And I've got a plan. I'm not just going to be working at some club at your age. I'm starting a company.

SAM: Doing what?

DARREN: Deejaying.

SAM: You're going backwards, Darren.

DARREN: Sam… Deejaying is a billion-dollar industry. People are always going to be getting married and throwing events. Even when the world completely shut down, people were still spending money on celebrations. People are always going to need music and people are always going to pay for music. I have all the equipment. I already do it for all our friends, so I know the setup. I know a ton of guys coming up looking to make some extra cash on the side.

I'm starting with weddings. In a year I'll branch out to graduations, proms, bar and bat mitzvahs. I have a business plan. I have a—

SAM: So, what's stopping you?

DARREN: I couldn't get a line of credit because of my student—

SAM: No father ever wants to hear that their daughter's boyfriend can't get a line of credit. Do you understand that?

DARREN: I couldn't get one for a while, but I did. Relax. I paid everything off. I don't have any debt. Hence the hundreds of jobs. And I just got a business loan. I've got everything I need to finally start.

SAM: So, you're going to do it?

DARREN: Yes. I've wanted to do this for ages.

SAM: Why have you never talked about any of this?

DARREN: Because you have never, ever asked.

Beat.

SAM: Hmmm.

DARREN: Hmmm? Hmmm? What Hmmm? What does that even mean?

SAM: No, it's… good. It's a good idea.

DARREN: I know it's a good idea. That's why I'm doing it.

SAM: Do you have a suit?

DARREN: Do I have a suit? Are you serious? You think I don't own a suit? You think I'm that much of a schmuck that I wouldn't have a—

SAM: Do you have a suit for tomorrow?

DARREN: You think I would show up knowing there was a wedding and not bring a suit? Yes, Sam… I have a suit.

SAM: Okay.

He takes a bite of ice cream and puts the lid on the tub.

Day 5

The next day.

The main floor of the house is decorated with beautiful floral arrangements. In the living room is a simple chuppah with a lace cloth over top. Under the chuppah is a music stand. All other furniture has been moved out of the room or pushed to the side to create space for the wedding party.

The room is empty.

From offstage we hear someone kicking off their shoes.

After a moment, RACHEL runs in. She's wearing her jacket and sweatsuit, but her hair and makeup are all done up.

RACHEL is clutching a plastic bag in her hand. She goes to the cupboard, grabs a glass, and fills it under the tap. She drinks and drinks and drinks.

SHELLEY runs into the kitchen from offstage. She's wearing her robe, slippers, and curlers. Her makeup is also done.

SHELLEY: Where have you been? We're starting any minute. Are you trying to make me have a heart attack?

RACHEL: I had to get something.

SHELLEY: Now?

RACHEL: Yes, now.

SHELLEY: What was so important that you had to run out moments before my wedding to—

As RACHEL starts to run the tap again, SHELLEY grabs the bag out of RACHEL's hand.

RACHEL: Shelley!

SHELLEY: Rachel!

RACHEL grabs the bag back.

RACHEL: Don't.

They hear voices coming from one of the rooms offstage.

RACHEL: Go! Go get ready!

SHELLEY: You go get ready!

The ladies sneak off to SHELLEY's bedroom while trying not to be seen. SAM and ELI walk into the living room dressed in suits. SAM walks with one cane and wears a flower on his lapel.

ELI: Do you need a hand?

SAM: No. No. I can do this.

ELI: Do you want a chair, at least?

SAM: I'm not sitting in a chair at my own wedding.

ELI: I don't want you putting yourself under any stress.

SAM: That's why we're going to make this quick.

DARREN comes in offstage dressed in a crisp suit. He is tuning a guitar.

You clean up well.

DARREN: I could say the same thing about you.

SAM: Did you bring that?

DARREN: I found it in your basement. Thought it was better than just playing some CD.

SAM: Thanks.

ELI: Sam, do you have the rings?

SAM: In my pocket. My heart's racing.

SHELLEY: *(Offstage.)* How much time do you need out there?

SAM: *(Calling back.)* How much time do you need in there?

SHELLEY: *(Offstage.)* We're ready.

SAM: *(Calling back.)* Well…

He looks at ELI and DARREN.

So are we.

SHELLEY: *(Offstage.)* So… Should we start?

Beat.

SAM: *(Calling back.)* Yes.

SHELLEY and RACHEL step out of the bedroom. RACHEL is wearing a dress that we haven't seen yet but looks fairly similar to the others she tried on. SHELLEY is dressed in a wedding gown. They both look wonderful.

SHELLEY: Do I have anything on my teeth?

She smiles wide for RACHEL to check.

RACHEL: No.

SHELLEY: Do you want me to check yours?

RACHEL: No.

She fixes SHELLEY's hair.

You look beautiful.

SHELLEY: So do you.

RACHEL puts SHELLEY's veil over her face.

SAM: *(Calling to them.)* Can we start?

RACHEL: *(Calling back)* Yes!

ELI nods to DARREN who starts to play the guitar. RACHEL walks into the living room, down a small aisle, and lands at the chuppah. Seconds later, SHELLEY walks the exact same path until she reaches SAM and stands beside him. SAM beams at the sight of her. DARREN finishes playing. SAM and SHELLEY turn to each other.

ELI: It is with great pleasure that today I attend the wedding of Sam and Shelley. We have come together to extend our support for their unique and special union. As a rabbi, I can offer my blessings for this marriage, and I can legalize it but ultimately only the two of you can make it real, enduring, and meaningful—

ELI looks at SAM and SHELLEY.

This language isn't right given the—

SAM: Eli, keep going.

SHELLEY: Continue, Eli. Please. It's beautiful.

ELI: Marriage symbolizes the intimate sharing of two lives, yet this sharing cannot be at the expense of either partner's individuality. It is within a loving relationship that we can often discover our own strengths.

The two of you met in the fall of 2013 when Shelley joined our congregation. From your first conversation, you were both smitten—realizing almost instantly how much you had in common. Your lives together started quickly and since then you haven't looked back.

You became engaged… well, two days ago. And have been planning this wedding now for… well, for two days. But it's clear that even this quick and deep expression of love has been handled with the same amount of care that you bring to every aspect of your relationship.

As you know, true love is caring behaviour that reinforces self-esteem, relieves pain, and always, offers support.

ELI: As a tribute to enduring love, I now invite Rachel to sing part of the Jewish folksong, "Erev Shel Shoshanim."

DARREN accompanies RACHEL on the guitar.

RACHEL: *(Singing.)* Erev shel shoshanim
Nitzeh na el habustan
Mor besamim ulevona Leraglech miftan.
Layla yored le'at
Veru'ach shoshan noshvah Havah elchash
lach shir balat Zemer shel ahav.

DARREN and RACHEL finish the song.

ELI: You have decided to forgo the tradition of lighting the candles and drinking of the wine so that—and I quote from Sam—"I don't fall asleep."

SHELLEY: Sam!

SAM: What? I'm old!

ELI: Sam and Shelley, we are about to validate your journey together as husband and wife. This ceremony is the bridge between your past and… and your future.

Rachel and Darren, Sam and Shelley are aware that it takes two people to create a couple, but that it requires help to create a marriage. Do you promise to be there for them and support them? If so, would you please say, "Yes, we do."

RACHEL/
DARREN: Yes, we do.

ELI: Sam and Shelley, would you face each other and take each other's hands.

They do.

ELI: Do you come of your own free will and without reservation to share your lives in marriage during painful as well as joyous times? If so, please say, "Yes, we do."

SAM/ SHELLEY: Yes, we do.

ELI: Could I have the rings, please?

SAM hands him the rings. ELI hands SAM SHELLEY's ring.

Sam, place this ring on Shelley's finger and repeat after me.

SAM places the ring on SHELLEY's finger.

Haray at m'uchadet iti,

SAM: Haray at m'uchadet iti,

ELI: b'tabaat zo,

SAM: b'tabaat zo,

ELI: b'ahava,

SAM: b'ahava,

ELI: u-b'neemanut.

SAM: u-b'neemanut.

ELI hands SHELLEY the ring. SHELLEY places the ring on SAM's finger.

ELI: Shelley, place this ring on Sam's finger and say in English, "Behold, with this ring."

SHELLEY: Behold, with this ring.

ELI: We are united in love and loyalty.

SHELLEY: We are united in love and loyalty.

DARREN hands ELI a tallit and then places a wrapped piece of glass at SAM and SHELLEY's feet.

ELI: Samuel Brian Adelman and Shelley Sarah Hoffman, you have freely committed yourselves to sharing your lives, and have exchanged rings in the presence of your loved ones as witnesses, thus joining yourselves in marriage. I, Rabbi Eli Limmer, rejoice to recognize you as husband and wife.

He wraps them both in the tallit.

Please break the glass together, then feel free to seal your marriage with a kiss.

DARREN places a covered glass near their feet and SHELLEY breaks it with her shoes.

Mazel tov!

DARREN plays "Siman Tov Mazel Tov" on the guitar and they all sing.

ALL: *(Singing.)* Siman tov u'mazal tov
U'mazal tov vesiman tov (x3)
Y'he lanu.

SAM and SHELLEY share a kiss. SAM takes SHELLEY's hand. As they start to walk down the aisle again, SAM begins to sway a bit.

SHELLEY: Are you all right?

SAM: I'm fine.

They take another step and SAM passes out. He falls instantly to the floor. Everyone runs to him.

SHELLEY: Sam!

RACHEL: Dad!

SHELLEY: Call 911! Call 911!

DARREN is already on his phone making the call. ELI gets closer and loosens SAM's tie.

Anything?

ELI checks for a pulse.

No, no, no. Sam!

RACHEL: Dad! Dad!

Day 6

The next morning.

RACHEL is fast asleep on the couch. DARREN enters the room. He watches her for a moment while she sleeps. She looks peaceful. DARREN gently shakes her arm to wake her.

DARREN: Rach.

RACHEL: What time is it?

DARREN: Late. We slept in. Were you here all night?

RACHEL: I fell asleep after the paramedics left.

DARREN: Have you seen Shelley or your dad?

RACHEL: Not since everyone went to bed.

She sits up and wipes the drool from her mouth.

DARREN: Yesterday was…

RACHEL: I know.

DARREN: One minute he was fine. And the next minute he—

RACHEL: I know.

DARREN: And we were trying to save him.

RACHEL: What?

DARREN: I'm just saying… Your dad's getting ready to end his life and we just spent the night trying to keep him alive.

RACHEL: Yeah. Right.

She moans and grabs her stomach.

DARREN: Are you okay?

He sees a garbage can near the couch.

RACHEL: I was throwing up most of the night.

DARREN: Why didn't you come and get me?

RACHEL: You were asleep.

DARREN: Let me get you some water.

RACHEL: I don't think that's going to help.

DARREN: You should go to your bed and get some more sleep.

RACHEL: I don't think I can get up.

DARREN: Do you want some help? Do you want me to carry you or—

RACHEL: No. No. Darren, you should… You should sit down. Sit.

DARREN sits close to her.

Grab that bag.

DARREN reaches over and hands her the plastic bag we saw her bring home earlier. She nods for him to open it.

I took six of them.

DARREN: Six?

RACHEL: I bought three and I was sure the results were wrong, so I went out and got three more.

DARREN: You're…

RACHEL nods her head "yes."

You're sure?

RACHEL nods her head "yes."

Is it… mine?

RACHEL: What? Yes, it's yours.

DARREN: I don't know. I don't know who you've been seeing since we—

RACHEL: I haven't been seeing anyone, Darren. Who have you been—

DARREN: I haven't seen anybody.

RACHEL: Also… it takes a little longer than that for all of this to happen.

DARREN: Right. Yeah. Sorry. I'm just…

Beat.

I mean… We've talked about it. We've talked about it a lot.

RACHEL: Talking about it and it happening are two very different things.

DARREN: I know. I…

He starts to smile and looks away from her.

RACHEL: What are you doing?

DARREN: Nothing.

RACHEL: What are… Are you smiling? Darren!

DARREN: I can't help it. It's kind of amazing… Isn't it?

RACHEL: Amazingly fucked up. We're not even together.

DARREN: I know that.

RACHEL: So?

DARREN: So… I mean… Think about it.

RACHEL: I am thinking about it. I can't stop thinking about it. It's all I'm thinking about.

DARREN: You're pregnant with our… How are you? How are you feeling?

Should you be sitting up right now?

RACHEL: Pregnant women sit up all the time, Darren. This is all so…

DARREN: Would it really be that bad?

RACHEL: It could be.

DARREN: But it could also be really… Can we not even be a little excited right now? Just like… a teeny, tiny bit—

RACHEL: I don't know what this means.

DARREN: Neither do I.

RACHEL: I don't know what this means for me… for us… I don't even know how long I would be around to even raise a child—

DARREN: What?

RACHEL: My mom was so young when she—

DARREN: Rachel.

RACHEL: She was so young and so sick. There's nothing to say that won't happen to me. There's nothing to say that I won't die early and that my child won't have to go through the same thing that I—

DARREN: Okay, yes, you don't know. We don't know. None of us know anything. But thinking about things that might never even happen… That's crazy.

RACHEL: No, Darren. That's what it means to be Jewish. We're always thinking about things that might never even happen. I just… I don't even know what to—

DARREN: Come here.

She crawls over to him on the couch, and he holds her tight.

I'm here. For all of it. Whatever you decide to do… Whatever we decide to do… I am here. I'm here for—

The bedroom door opens. SHELLEY shuffles across the floor in her robe and slippers. Her hair is a mess.

RACHEL: How is he?

SHELLEY: Well, he's awake. But he's not… He's not well. He's really not…

RACHEL breathes deeply and bends over.

DARREN: Are you going to be sick again?

RACHEL: I don't know.

SHELLEY: Oh, don't start that now.

RACHEL: I'm not doing it on purpose.

DARREN rubs her back.

SHELLEY: What's wrong with her?

DARREN: She's… under the weather.

RACHEL groans.

SHELLEY: Is it the flu? Because your father cannot catch anything. It will actually kill him if he—

RACHEL: He won't catch this. Trust me.

SHELLEY looks at RACHEL and then at DARREN.

SHELLEY: Is she…

DARREN looks at SHELLEY.

Rachel, are you…

RACHEL: Yes, Shelley. I am.

SHELLEY: Does this mean… Oh my god. Oh my god. I'm going to be a bubbie.

RACHEL: Shelley!

SHELLEY: I have always wanted to be a bubbie!

SAM: *(From bedroom.)* Shelley?

SHELLEY: Oh, he better not be getting up. *(Calling out.)* Sam! Sam!

She goes to check on SAM.

DARREN: Do you want to go back to bed? Do you want to—

RACHEL: I should tell him.

DARREN: What? Tell him what?

RACHEL: I should tell my dad. About this. About—

DARREN: Woah, woah, woah. We don't know what we're doing yet. We should figure that out first before you tell anyone that you're—

RACHEL: There has to be a reason though, right? A reason why this is happening... why this is happening now. Maybe this is it. Maybe this is the thing that will actually change his—

SHELLEY comes out of the bedroom.

SHELLEY: He got up to use the bathroom. I told him to go back to bed.

RACHEL: I'm going to tell him.

DARREN: Don't.

She heads toward the bedroom and DARREN grabs her hand to stop her.

RACHEL shakes DARREN off her.

RACHEL: He should know.

DARREN: No. No. He shouldn't.

SHELLEY: What?!

DARREN: *(To SHELLEY.)* She wants to tell him that she's—

SHELLEY: No. No. Don't. Don't do that.

She grabs RACHEL'S hand and pulls her back.

RACHEL: Oww.

SHELLEY: No!

RACHEL: You were practically about to start picking out baby clothes and you don't want me telling him that I'm—

SHELLEY: Rachel, you are not telling your father anything.

She goes to the bedroom and shuts the door.

Under no circumstances are you to tell your—

RACHEL: He has a right to know—

DARREN: Yeah. When we decide what we're actually going to do here.

SHELLEY: You can't say anything to him. You can't.

RACHEL: I don't actually need permission... From either of you.

SHELLEY: Rachel!

RACHEL: He might decide not to go through with it. This could make all the difference. Don't you understand that? This could—

SHELLEY: Your father won't make it another nine months. It is not fair to tell him—

RACHEL: I have an actual reason why Dad would actually want to continue to… why he would want to continue to… He's always wanted grandchildren. He's amazing with kids. He—

SHELLEY: And what do you think his life as a grandfather is going to look like? Do you think he's going to be playing on the ground? Crawling around on his hands and knees? I understand why you want him to know. I do. But telling him would be for you. For you. It wouldn't be for—

The door to the bedroom opens. SAM walks into the room very, very slowly. He seems very groggy. He holds onto the wall as he walks for support. SHELLEY goes to him and helps him.

Where are your canes? You shouldn't be walking around without them.

SAM: I don't know.

SHELLEY: You just used them to go to the bathroom.

SAM: I couldn't find them.

SHELLEY: You shouldn't be walking around at all. The paramedics said you need to stay in bed.

SAM: What are you fighting about?

SHELLEY: It's nothing you have to be concerned about.

SAM: Is it about me?

SHELLEY: No, love. It's—

SAM takes another few steps forward then stops and closes his eyes.

SAM: I think I have to go back to bed.

SHELLEY: Good. Good idea. I'll take you.

RACHEL watches as SHELLEY takes SAM back to the bedroom.

RACHEL: Dad!

SAM stops and turns around. For the first time RACHEL sees how truly frail her father is.

SHELLEY looks at her, doing everything she can to beg RACHEL just by looking at her not to say anything.

Let me help.

She takes SAM'S other arm, and they walk him back to the bedroom.

Day 6

Later that night.

SAM and ELI sit in the living room together. SAM has a blanket wrapped around him.

ELI: I've been praying for you to die.

SAM: You wouldn't be the first person to say that to me. I think a couple of old girlfriends feel the same way.

ELI: Because if you die… and die naturally… then I can be there to perform any blessing or ritual you want. But…

Beat.

ELI: I called my mentor in Chicago... Rabbi Schwartz... I asked him what he would do if he was in my position.

SAM: And? What did your Rabbi Schwartz have to say?

ELI: First, he told me to get used to this kind of conversation. Because people are only getting older and only getting more ill. And they're living longer. And so, this will be a big challenge for us... For rabbis in the next few years. How do we help those in our congregations with this? And in this way if this is what they are requesting? And then he said... Is your friend ill? I said yes. Of course, he's ill. And then he said... But is he terminally ill? And I said not terminally. You can move, you can walk, you can eat, you can swallow.

SAM: Barely.

ELI: And then he said... Is your friend in palliative care? And I said no. But that you will likely need to be if this goes on much longer. He said is he mentally sound? I said from everything I can tell, yes. Though he's always had a screw loose or two.

SAM: Or three.

ELI: And then he said... Is he suffering? Is he in pain? Is he in discomfort? Is he unable to go on? Is there any hope of a recovery?

Beat.

I need to know... I need you to look me in the eyes and tell me... Are you suffering in a way that you have never suffered before? Can you really not go on any longer like this? I know you're tired. I know you're in pain. But are you suffering? Because if you are… Then maybe I can wrap my mind around all of this. And don't just say you are because I'm asking. I need to know. I need to know—

SAM: Why would I be doing this if I wasn't?

ELI: People have all kinds of reasons for doing things.

SAM: As Jews, our traditions insist that the preservation of human life must override virtually every other religious rule or law, correct?

ELI: In some cases, correct.

SAM: And as Jews, our traditions also insist that relieving pain and allowing for the soul to have a peaceful departure is of the utmost importance, correct?

ELI: Correct.

SAM: I am ready to be without pain. I am ready to not cause pain to those around me.

ELI: You don't.

SAM: Not yet. But I will. And it will only get worse. No matter what they make me take or what they make me do… it's all downhill from here, Eli. And watching someone you love disintegrate before your very eyes… I did it with Barbara. I watched her entire life just slip away from her. I'm not doing that. I'm not doing that to them… And I'm not doing that to me. I am done. I am done with the pain. I am done with the suffering. I am ready for a peaceful departure.

ELI: I've never been in the room before. I've been present after someone has passed on… Many, many times. But I have never been present for an actual death before. Not like this. What if I'm not good at it? Especially considering it will be you. What if I'm not… What if I can't…

SAM: Hey… Have a little faith.

ELI: All right. All right. I'll be there. All right.

SAM reaches out his hand to ELI. ELI takes it and squeezes it tight.

SAM: I need you to get something for me. *(Pointing to a table.)* In the top drawer.

ELI goes to a table and opens the drawer. He pulls out a large envelope.

In there you'll find all of the funeral arrangements. I've left everything for Shelley, too, but just in case… Now you have it. It's all there. No one should lift a finger. Just do what is there and everything will be taken care of.

ELI: You have no idea how many people refuse to make plans and just let their families take care of it after they're gone.

SAM: It's the least I can do, given what I'm putting everyone through.

ELI: I don't have any of this organized for myself. I'm so busy dealing with other people dying. I don't even know what I would want. Or how I would want to—

SAM: If you don't mind me suggesting… Maybe give it a think. So that someone doesn't go ahead and decide for you.

ELI: I guess I have some homework to do.

SAM: You sure do.

ELI: You've always been one step ahead of me.

SAM: Eli, I can barely walk.

ELI: Still…

SAM: Still. Oh… I'm leaving you my baseball cards. All of them. We both know I always had the better collection.

ELI: Well, the joke's on you. Now I have the better collection.

ELI stands and turns for the door.

SAM: Hey…

ELI looks at him.

Thank you.

ELI nods his head, smiles, and leaves. SAM is alone in the room.

SAM closes his eyes. The door to the bedroom opens and SHELLEY walks into the room.

SHELLEY: You should be in bed.

SAM: I'll be there soon.

SHELLEY: Is he going to do it?

SAM: He is.

SHELLEY sits near SAM and grabs his hand.

SHELLEY: Some honeymoon.

SAM: I'll say.

SHELLEY: Sammy…

Beat.

What am I going to do in this house without you?

SAM: Oh, you'll throw parties. Have all your friends over.

SHELLEY: What am I going to do in this city without you?

SAM: You'll go to all of our favourite places. And you'll find new places.

SHELLEY: And what am I going to do without you?

SAM: You will be perfectly fine. Maybe not at first—

SHELLEY: Not ever.

SAM: But you will. Shelley… You can date when I'm gone. You can meet people. You can fall in love. You can get married.

SHELLEY: How can you even say something like that?

SAM: I realized we haven't talked about this yet. And it's important that you know that I want you to be happy.

SHELLEY: I'm happy with you. I want you. I don't want anyone else.

SAM: But if you meet someone else… That would be a good thing. You have many, many years ahead of you.

SHELLEY: Are you trying to get rid of me?

SAM: No. But if the tables were turned, wouldn't you want me to meet someone else?

SHELLEY: No. Absolutely not. I'd want you to miss me like crazy each and every day. I'd want you to torture yourself with how much you missed me.

SAM: Well, that goes without saying. But I want you to know that it's okay, Shell. Truly.

SHELLEY: I don't even know what day garbage day is. I don't know how to fix the toilet when it runs. I don't know how to get the security alarm to stop going off. I don't know the code to get into the garage.

SAM: Okay, okay. I need you to get something for me. *(Pointing to a table.)* In the top drawer.

SHELLEY goes to a table and opens the drawer. She pulls out a small binder.

In there, you'll find everything you need. The garbage schedules. I've left all the information for our home insurance. I've written out instructions for the security system. And I've changed the code to the garage to the day and month of our wedding.

SAM: And I left you the number of our handyman because I have never fixed a toilet in my life. And if you have any issues with the house… Call Darren.

SHELLEY: Darren? When did that happen?

SAM: Sometimes things change when things change.

SHELLEY goes to him and hugs SAM tightly. After a moment, RACHEL walks into the room.

RACHEL: Is she okay?

SHELLEY: No!

SAM holds her.

SAM: She's going to be. *(To SHELLEY.)* Shell… Why don't you get changed and we'll go for a walk?

SHELLEY: You can't go for a walk.

SAM: Why don't you get changed and we'll sit outside?

SHELLEY: Do you just want me to leave so you two can talk?

SAM: Yes, sweetheart. I do.

SHELLEY: Okay.

She kisses the top of SAM's head. Then leaves the room so SAM and RACHEL can speak.

SAM: You're going to need to keep an eye on her. Don't lose touch with her, all right? She's family.

RACHEL: Technically, she's not—

SAM: Rachel… She's family.

Beat.

I need you to get something for me. *(Pointing to a table.)* In the top drawer.

RACHEL goes to a table and opens the drawer. She pulls out a small envelope.

There are some details in there that I need a lawyer to deal with. It can be you if you want. If not, your cousin Noah is awaiting your call. I left his number in there for you. I'm leaving you some money—

RACHEL: Dad—

SAM: Let me finish. I'm leaving you some money. I hope it's enough to help you put a down payment on something. I'm leaving some for the Temple and a few other organizations. But it's a large enough amount to help you out down the road. I'm leaving some to Shelley. And I'm leaving her the house.

RACHEL: I thought you would.

SAM: I figure you don't want to move here and live here. And I don't want to uproot Shelley for no reason.

RACHEL: It's good. It's the right choice. You know you don't have to leave me anything, right?

SAM: I know that but… Tough luck. I'm going to.

RACHEL: Thank you. And I'll do whatever you need me to do. Whatever you've left me to…

Beat.

RACHEL goes to him and kneels at his feet.

RACHEL: Dad... I'm...

Beat.

You can still back out. You know that, don't you? You don't have to do this. You really, really don't. You can call this whole thing off. You can call it off right now. Please. Dad. Don't do this. Don't. Please don't. Please. Please don't do this. Don't. I'm begging you. Please don't. Don't do this. Please. Don't do this. Please. Please. Please. Don't. Don't do this.

SAM looks at her. RACHEL puts her head on his knee and rests it there for a moment. After a while, she gets up.

I'm going to see if Shelley wants me to prep anything for dinner.

RACHEL leaves. SAM sits alone in the living room.

Day 7

The next morning.

SAM is lying in his bed. He is dressed in his favourite sweatsuit. He wears a kippah. RACHEL and SHELLEY stand near the bed. ELI is preparing. He is wearing his tallit and kippah.

SHELLEY: Are you comfortable?

SAM: Does it matter?

SHELLEY: Sam!

SAM: I'm comfortable. I've never been more comfortable in my entire life.

DARREN walks into the room. He is also wearing a kippah.

DARREN: The doctor just arrived.

SAM: He's early. I like that in a doctor.

SHELLEY starts to cry. SAM takes her hand.

Can someone untuck me a bit? I'm overheating.

DARREN untucks the sheets.

Thank you again for helping with the... thing.

DARREN: Yeah. Of course.

RACHEL: What thing?

SAM: Never mind.

RACHEL: What thing?

SAM: You'll see.

RACHEL: See what?

DARREN: Don't worry about it.

RACHEL: What are you two talking about?

SAM: It's okay. You'll see.

DARREN: Should I call the doctor in?

ELI: Let's have him wait in the living room.

DARREN: I'll tell him.

DARREN leaves to speak to the doctor. SAM pulls on RACHEL's hand.

SAM: He's a good one.

RACHEL: What?

SAM: I want you to know... He's a good one.

RACHEL: You want to do this now?

SAM: When else am I going to do it?

RACHEL: Okay.

SAM: He's good.

ELI: Are you ready?

SAM: As ready as I'm going to be.

ELI: Sam?

SAM: Yes. I'm ready.

DARREN comes back in.

DARREN: He says to call him in when we're...

ELI: All right. Let's all gather around the bed.

RACHEL, SHELLEY, ELI, and DARREN gather around SAM.

Before we gathered, Sam and I said the Viduy together. The returning of one's soul to God at the end of its journey in this world is probably the most profound moment in a person's life. It is for this purpose that our sages prepared the Viduy... Our confession... To be recited before one... Before one departs. It is usually said in private so that the person... So that the person who is facing their death may recite it with a clear mind and heart. And now that we have done that...

The final prayer to be said is of course the Shema. I will sing it. Then Sam. Then we may all sing together.

He closes his eyes.

(Singing.) Shema Yisrael Adonai eloheinu Adonai ehad.

SAM: *(Singing.)* Shema Yisrael Adonai eloheinu Adonai ehad.

ALL: *(Singing.)* Shema Yisrael Adonai eloheinu Adonai ehad.

ELI: *(Singing.)* Amayn.

SAM takes a moment and looks at each person in the room directly in the eyes. This should last as long as it needs to.

The room is completely still. SAM looks at ELI and nods.

All right. You can… You can bring him in.

Epilogue

Later that day.

RACHEL sits alone in the living room, lost in thought. Then she hears her phone ping. The sound snaps her back into the room. She opens her phone and sees an email in her inbox. The email has a voice file. She plays it.

DARREN: 1, 2, 3.

On the recording, DARREN starts to strum "I Just Called to Say I Love You" on the guitar. Then SAM sings the first two verses and the chorus of the song for RACHEL.

The recording stops. RACHEL sits alone for a long moment. After a while, SHELLEY comes out of the bedroom. Her eyes are red and puffy. She sits on the couch beside RACHEL.

RACHEL: Did you get enough time in there?

SHELLEY: No. But they have to take him now. If you want to go back in now is your chance.

RACHEL: I don't know if I can.

SHELLEY: Me neither. They might have to take me with him if I do. I can't get over how much he looks like he's just sleeping. He looks like any moment he could just open his eyes again and…

She looks around the room.

There are so many flowers. I didn't think about what it would be like to have all these flowers in here.

RACHEL: Do you want me to get rid of them?

SHELLEY: No. I'll keep them. I like the reminder. Plus, they weren't cheap. The dresses! I have fifteen dresses draped around your father's office. I have to return them to the mall. I should go return them to the—

RACHEL: It's okay. We'll go later… Tomorrow. We can go together.

She places her hand on her stomach.

Have you eaten?

SHELLEY: No. I haven't eaten in days.

RACHEL: Are you hungry?

SHELLEY: I could eat. Do you want me to make us something?

RACHEL: I can do it. What do we have?

SHELLEY: Bagels. Lots and lots of poppy seed bagels. They're in the freezer.

No one at Temple would eat them so I brought them all home with us. I suppose I'll be eating poppy seed bagels for the rest of my life.

RACHEL smiles. They sit on the couch together in silence for a moment. Then RACHEL reaches out and touches SHELLEY'S hand. They don't look at each other. They sit there in silence together. Neither is able to pull themselves off the couch. At least, not yet.

End of play.

Study Guide

Adapted from the study guide resource compiled by Grand Theatre Education Department, Breanne Ritchie (britchie@grandtheatre.com) and Danielle Dixon (ddixon@grandtheatre.com)

Themes

- Coping with grief and loss
- Family strength
- Medical assistance in dying (MAID), faith, and ethics
- Honouring end of life decisions

Synopsis

- DAY 1: Rachel returns to her family home in London, Ontario to visit her dad, Sam, and his partner, Shelley, for the weekend. When Rachel arrives, she's greeted by Shelley, who begins to question her about her recent breakup and the six dozen poppy seed bagels that she brought with her. In the middle of their heated conversation, Sam shuffles into the room and greets his daughter, Rachel. As Rachel and Sam catch up, Shelley begins to make comments that suggest something is going on. Sam reveals that the cancer he once had is now in his prostate and spreading. Tired from the pain, and not wanting to go through chemotherapy again, Sam has made the decision to end his life through medical assistance in dying (MAID), which will happen in seven days. Devastated and confused by what her father is telling her, Rachel refuses to believe that MAID is the only option.

- DAY 2: After staying up all night and researching doctors and new procedures for her father, Rachel ends up falling asleep at the kitchen table. She's abruptly woken up by Shelley banging a pot over her head. As Shelley and Rachel begin to bicker, Rachel receives a phone call from her now ex-boyfriend, Darren, who tells her of a new Facebook post her father has created. Rachel is horrified as she reads the online post—it publicly announces her father's intention to use MAID. The phones begin to ring with calls from concerned friends. Rachel begins to tell her father about an oncologist in Buffalo who has success with cancer patients like him, but Sam has made up his mind. Mid-conversation, Rachel is struck by a wave of nausea and dizziness.

- DAY 3: Rachel convinces Eli, Sam's rabbi and childhood friend, to come to the house and talk Sam out of medical assistance in dying. Eli and Sam reminisce about the past and discuss the decision Sam has made. Eli, as a Reform rabbi and a good friend, is having trouble supporting Sam; MAID goes against their Jewish faith. Because of this, Eli is unable to agree to Sam's request to be present and give a blessing when Sam passes. Shelley is surprised when Sam takes out a ring box and proposes to her. Eli does agree to Sam's second request, which is to marry the couple in two days.

- DAY 4: While Rachel tries on pink dresses that Shelley has picked out for her to wear to the wedding, the two women get into a heated discussion. Rachel admits that she doesn't want Shelley to marry her father and that she is skeptical about Shelley's motives for being with her father. In the middle of the argument, Darren arrives. Later that night, Sam goes into the kitchen for some ice cream, only to find Darren sitting at the kitchen table. Knowing that Sam has never liked him, Darren is determined to resolve their differences once and for all. After their talk, the two men find new respect for one another.

- DAY 5: The house is decorated with flowers for Sam and Shelley's wedding. Rachel is the maid of honour, Darren plays the guitar, and Eli is the officiant. As the ceremony ends and the newlyweds walk down the aisle, Sam suddenly passes out and falls to the floor. The family calls 911.

- DAY 6: The next morning, Rachel is asleep on the couch when Darren gently wakes her up; he is concerned that she is not feeling well. Rachel admits to Darren that she took six pregnancy tests the previous day and they were all positive. Later that day, Sam and Eli sit in the living room and continue their conversation about the conflict of their faith and MAID. Eli has done some reflection, and he tells Sam that he will be present when he passes and will give the Jewish prayer of death as a blessing. After Eli leaves, Sam talks to both Shelley and Rachel about what will happen after he dies.

- DAY 7: Rachel, Shelley, Darren, and Eli are all gathered around Sam's bed. Eli sings the Shema, and then recites the El Maleh Rahamim prayer as Sam passes peacefully. Later that day, Rachel tries to come to terms with what has happened.

She receives an email that contains a voice file. Darren has recorded Sam singing "I Just Called to Say I Love You," the song he always sang to comfort Rachel when she was a little girl.

Research Questions

1. Not all countries have legalized medical assistance in dying. What led to the legalization of MAID in Canada?
2. How many people in Canada have used MAID since it began in 2016?
3. Who can access MAID? What are the eligibility criteria surrounding who can receive it?

Here is Health Canada's website page about MAID, which can help you to learn more:

https://www.canada.ca/en/health-canada/services/health-services-benefits/medical-assistance-dying.html

Discussion Questions

1. Why might someone choose to die using MAID?
2. Is MAID murder? Is it suicide? Why or why not?
3. What is the difference between unexpected loss and expected loss? Will a family member or a friend go through a different grieving process depending on the kind of loss?
4. Imagine that someone you know has decided to pursue medical assistance in dying. Would you try to talk them out of it? Why or why not?

Questions About the Play

1. Do you think Rachel's reasons for opposing Sam's plan to have medical assistance in dying were good ones or selfish ones?
2. Why do you think Sam proposed to Shelley when he knew that he would only be alive for a few more days?
3. Why did Eli change his mind about being present when Sam passed?
4. Why did Sam change his opinion about Darren?
5. Do you think that Rachel was right not to tell Sam that she was pregnant?
6. Do you think that the voice file Rachel receives at the end of the play will help her to process her grief?

Writing Exercise

Often when someone close to us dies, we regret the fact that we left things unsaid. One way to work through this kind of regret is to write a letter to the deceased person.

Is there anyone you have lost that you would like to express your feelings to? Take some time to write to that person now and tell them everything you wish you had said while they were alive.

If you haven't experienced the loss of someone close to you, write to someone who is living, and tell them honestly how you feel about them.